WAR DIARY

OF

RAF POCKLINGTON

BY

MIKE USHERWOOD

A WARTIME RECORD OF HEAVY BOMBER OPERATIONS

FROM A YORKSHIRE AIRFIELD 1941-45

A WAR DIARY

OF

RAF POCKLINGTON

1941-45

BY

MIKE USHERWOOD

Typeset using Ventura Publisher Gem version 3
Fonts used Times and Courier

Published in the United Kingdom by Compaid Graphics
Little Ash, Street Lane, Lower Whitley, Warrington, Cheshire. WA4 4EN

ISBN 0 9517965 2 6

Library Cataloguing Data

RAF Pocklington

First Edition August 1993

Photo Credits

Photographs on pages 10,34,36,43,59,133,208,216 taken by Author.
Thanks to B.V. Svenson for aerial photograhs, plane piloted by Author, Cessna 150
R.L.Mclean (McLean Aviation Rufforth) page 216

DEDICATION

To all members of Bomber Command who served in the last war. The Aircrew, volunteers all, who had a slightly less than even chance of survival.

To the Ground Crews who kept the aircraft flying often under the most uncomfortable conditions this book is respectfully dedicated.

FOREWORD

by Air Vice Marshal S O Bufton CB DFC FRAeS

On 12 April 1941, I took half of No. 10 Squadron (Whitleys) from RAF Leeming to form No 76 Squadron (Halifaxes) at RAF Linton-on- Ouse. We were converted and 'ready to go' on 14 May 1941 when hydraulic failures grounded all Halifaxes indefinitely. So, on 29 May 1941, I took command of the new clutch of airfields at Pocklington, Melbourne and Elvington. All this happened over 50 years ago, though it seems like yesterday. Please read on......

This is a remarkable book, meticulously researched and compiled, which tells the story of operations from Pocklington over 4 years of the Second World War (1941-45). From its pages one can sense the high achievement and the unspeakable gallantry of those brilliant young men who repeatedly, and without question, and mostly against the odds, risked their lives in the cause of freedom.

The story of Pocklington is, in effect, a microcosm of the whole of Bomber Command's offensive against Hitler. It reveals the severity of operations at various phases of the war, such as the battles of the Ruhr, of Hamburg and of Berlin, and, later, the comparative ease of passage once the invasion had rolled over Germany's early warning system and diminished her air defence capability.

This book is a story of great achievement, of sacrifice, and of the debt we owe to all those who took off on operations from the runways of Pocklington.

S O Bufton

Reigate
April 1992

Air Vice Marshal Bufton
(Died 29 March 1993 aged 85)

I have compiled this book mainly from the official records of that time, particularly from the Operations Record Books of R.A.F. Pocklington and also those of Numbers 405 and 102 Squadrons, but my thanks are due to:-

The helpful and patient staff of the Public Records Office, Kew.
The equally helpful staff at the Air Historical Branch of the Ministry of Defence and the R.A.F. Museum, Hendon.

Martin Middlebrook for permission to use the information contained in his and Chris Everitts masterly "Bomber Command War Diaries."

To the Bodley Head Publishers for permission to use John Pudney's Poem "Security."

To Dr. Jan Van Loewen Limited for permission to use Noel Cowards "Lie in the dark and listen."

To Ronald A.M. Ransom for permission to use the poem on Page 80 to the Methuen Company for permission to use Herbert Corby's poem "The Lost."

To Carol Reeves for typing the initial work and Sandy Williams and Heather Norrison for completing the work and not least for not grumbling at my handwriting.

To Steve Malcolm for loan of a Word Processor and showing me how to use it.

To Tom James, Keith Ford and Mike Mansfield for their help with the printing and publication and to the members of the Yorkshire Air Museum for their help.

To all my friends at the Worlds Gliding Club and the Hull Aero Club for putting up with me while I was working on this book.

It should be realised that this book has been compiled from the official records. These may not always be totally accurate especially in small details. They were written under pressure by people who had other things on their minds than achieving total accuracy for the benefit of latter-day researchers. If therefore I have given somebody the incorrect rank or worse still spelt their name wrong I can only offer my humble apologies.

Mike Usherwood

SECURITY

Empty your pockets, Tom, Dick and Harry,
Strip your identity; leave it behind.
Lawyer, Garage Hand, Grocer, Don't tarry,
With your own country, your own kind.

Leave all your letters, Suburb and Township,
Green-fen and grocery slip-way and bay,
Hot-spring and prairie, smoke-stack and coal-tip,
Leave in our keeping, while you're away.

Tom, Dick and Harry plain names and numbers,
Pilot, observer, and gunner depart,
Their personal litter only encumbers,
Somebody's head, somebody's heart.

John Pudney.

(Ten Summers Poems 1933-1943 Bodley Head.)

 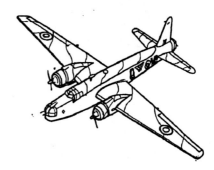

The Canadians are Coming

1941

By middle of 1941 it was obvious that the war was going to be a long hard struggle. Churchill's 'Blood Toil Tears and Sweat' had become a grim reality.

Though the country seemed safe from invasion following the hard won victory of Fighter Command the war was not going well. On land Rommel had retaken most of North Africa, Greece amd Crete had fallen. At sea the Axis blockade was beginning to take hold and although the Bismark had been sunk the Hood had been lost in the same action. At home the blitz was still continuing. London and most big cities were subject to air attacks most nights.

The only force we had capable of taking the war to the enemy was Bomber Command. From it's small beginnings in 1939 it slowly developed into one of the most devastating forces ever mounted. This is the story of one of those Airfields which took part in one of the longest and hardest battles ever fought.

The Station opened on the 5th May 1941 when F/O Street and party reported followed by a "Working-Up" party 10 days later.

On the 20th May 1941 the "Opening-Up" party arrived and Group Captain S.O. Bufton D.F.C. was posted in as Station Commander from 76 Squadron at R.A.F. Linton-on-Ouse.

No 405 Squadron R.C.A.F. arrived from R.A.F. Driffield on the 20th June under the Command of Wing Commander P.A. Gilchrist with 16 Wellington Mk II aircraft of which 6 were fit for operations. There were 8 crews operational and also another 10 crews on leave.

Pocklington Base 27/04/1942
RCHM Copyright

The night of 22/23 June 1941 saw the first air operation launched from Pocklington. Eight aircraft were ordered to attack Wilhelmshaven, one did not start, 2 returned early with engine trouble and one jettisoned its bombs, unable to find the target. However according to German records no bombs fell on Wilhelmshaven on this night. All aircraft reported considerable searchlight activity but the only intense flak was near the coast. Two aircraft reported being fired on by a convoy as they neared the British coast on return and one had a parachute set on fire but jettisoned it successfully.

The first aircraft to take off was W 5476 at 2310 hours the crew being Sergeants Richard, Allison, Skan, Murfin, James and Corfield. They reported over the target at 01.40 bombing from 13,000 ft and landed at 04.38.

8

25th-26th June 1941

Girmania Submarine Works at Kiel. Eight aircraft were detailed. One returned early with engine trouble and bought it's bombs back, 5 bombed the target reporting that the flak on this occasion was not as heavy as usual

Of the remaining aircraft, one bombed Renasburgh and the other Tonning, as neither aircraft was able to locate the target due to haze. The aircraft which bombed Tonning had its petrol pump go unserviceable as well as 2 turret recuperators forcing the crew to pump for 4 hours.

2nd-3rd July, 1941

Cologne. 9 aircraft. One returned early with engine trouble and one was forced to jettison, also with engine trouble and then got lost, finally landing at Wittering. Of the remainder, 6 bombed the main railway station and one Cologne itself. Fires and explosions were seen in the city. The flak on this occasion diminished during the attack.

4th-5th July, 1941

Brest. 9 aircraft. All bombed the dock area and the battleship Prince Eugen before smoke screen became effective. Opposition weak.

6th-7th July, 1941

Dortmund. 10 aircraft. One did not start and 1 returned early due to a loose engine cowling. 6 bombed the target and one Dusseldorf due to faulty navigational equipment and one Wessel for the same reason. One aircraft was attacked by an ME110 but drove it off. Flak was fairly intensive but numerous searchlights appeared to be used to indicate course of aircraft.

One aircraft (D) returned on one engine which caught fire on the approach. The pilot (F/O Fraas) attempted to gain height but the aircraft crashed near the airfield. The rear-gunner (F/S Luckhurst) was killed and F/O Fraas died the next day. The rest of the crew P/O O'Brien, Sergeant's McKernan, Brown and Doyle were badly injured.

F/O Fraas is buried in Hitchin cemetery.

F/S Luckhurst is buried in Farnham cemetery. At the time of his death his son, Robert, was 11 months old.

Rotterdam. One "Freshman" aircraft. This crew succeeded in straddling the target (Oil Tanks). Moderate flak.

Grave of F/O Fraas at Hitchin   Grave of F/S Luckhurst

7th-8th July, 1941

Osnabruck. 9 aircraft. 2 returned early with engine and turret trouble. 2 lost their way in spite of perfect weather and believed they had bombed Munster. The rest made a successful attack but damage was only slight.

9th July, 1941

One aircraft damaged when it taxied into soft ground. This caused the tail to rise and then drop heavily.

9th-10th July, 1941

Aachen. 8 aircraft. One did not start and one bombed Cologne, running into intense flak and searchlights.

The remainder reported that the target had been left a mass of flames. Flak "subnormal." Searchlights numerous but ineffective.

Owing to mist at base, all aircraft diverted on return landing at Dishforth, Yeadon, Abingdon, Upper Heyford and Benson.

13th July, 1941

One aircraft ran off perimeter track into soft ground, damaging airscrew.

14th July, 1941

The station was visited by the Air Officer Commanding No 4 Group, Air Vice Marshal Coningham.

14th-15th July, 1941

Hannover. 8 aircraft. One returned early with unserviceable rear turret. Crews were unable to pinpoint the target owing to bad haze and a large number of dummy fires. However, all crews claimed to have bombed the vicinity of the target and observed many fires.

One aircraft (N) did not return. The crew, Sergeant Thrower, P/O Morgan, Sergeant's Slaughter, Jones, Kirk and Dosseter all became Prisoners of War.

Rotterdam. 2 "Freshman" aircraft. Successful operation.

15 July, 1941

A sea search for Sgt. Throwers aircraft, missing from the previous night's operation, was abandoned due to bad weather.

17th July, 1941

The station was visited by the A.O.C. Bomber Command, Air Marshal Sir Richard Pierce KCB DSO MC.

21st-22nd July, 1941

Frankfurt. 8 aircraft. One returned early with engine trouble. 6 reached and attacked the target and one bombed Ostend owing to W.T. failure.

One aircraft reported seeing a V on the ground north of Brussels with arms 100 yards long, like a huge neon sign and one aircraft had an inconclusive combat with a night fighter.

24th July, 1941

Gneisenau in Brest Dock. 9 aircraft. This was a daylight operation and met considerable opposition. Sgt. Craig's aircraft was badly damaged and the rear gunner wounded but shot down 2 of the 4 fighters which attacked it. This aircraft returned at sea level with all the crew in the tail to compensate for the damage and ditched successfully 300 yards from the coast, all the crew being picked up by a motor boat. One other aircraft claimed to have shot down a fighter.

One other aircraft was attacked by an ME 109, badly wounding the rear gunner (Sgt. Darnley). This aircraft crash landed at Roborough (Plymouth) but Sgt. Darnley died later in hospital.

Two aircraft did not return including one flown by the Squadron Commander W/C Gilchrist.

W/C Gilchrist, DFC. Taken Prisoner, but escaped to Switzerland and returned to the U.K.
Sgt. Paton Evaded capture and returned via Gibralter.
P/O MacKay Prisoner of War.
Sgt. Westbury Prisoner of War.
Sgt. Dalphond Evaded capture and returned via Gibralter.
F/O Wighan Killed.

P/O Truman Killed.
Sgt. Crump Killed.
Sgt. Mitchell Killed.
Sgt. Fawkes Killed.
Sgt. Tatton Killed.
Sgt. Martin Killed.

30th July, 1941

One aircraft damaged when it taxied into contractor's tractor.

30th-31st July, 1941

Cologne. 6 aircraft. One returned early with unserviceable air speed indicator. The rest attacked a flak concentration on E.T.A. Heavy cloud made the result of this operation doubtful. Of a total of 116 aircraft despatched, only 3 H.E. and about 300 incendiaries fell on Cologne.

Boulogne. 1 "Freshman" aircraft. Forced to jettison in heavy cloud.

2nd-3rd August, 1941

Berlin. 7 aircraft. The target was successfully attacked but the aiming point (Railway Station) could not be identified due to haze. Aircraft were able to navigate by means of fires at Texel and Den Helder as well as flak at Aldenburg, Hannover and Emden. One aircraft bombed Bremen owing to a rough engine and high fuel consumption. Searchlights numerous with flak co-operating.

One aircraft did not return.

(J)

F/L Kipp Prisoner of War.
P/O Terry Prisoner of War.
Sgt. Skan Prisoner of War.
Sgt. Murfin Prisoner of War.
Sgt. Pruette Prisoner of War.
Sgt. Menzies Prisoner of War.

(F)

P/O Cox Killed.
P/O Horn Killed.
P/O Learmouth Killed.
Sgt. Thomas Killed.
Sgt. Reed Killed.
Sgt. McKenzie Killed.

Hamburg. 1 "Freshman" aircraft. Did not return.

5th-6th August, 1941

Karlsruhe. 6 aircraft. 2 did not start and one had to jettison following an encounter with an ME 110. One was also forced to bomb Aachen due to engine trouble. The remaining 2 attacked the target and reported the Infantry Barracks in the Waldestrasse the centre of a large blaze. Opposition weak.

A "Freshman" operation with 2 aircraft was cancelled.

7th-8th August, 1941

Dortmund. 9 aircraft including 3 "Freshman". 8 bombed the target and one Witten. One aircraft cruised for an hour before identifying the target but then managed to straddle the railway yards. One aircraft encountered 4 night fighters but got away after exchanging shots and taking violent avoiding action.

12th-13th August, 1941

Berlin. 9 aircraft. 2 returned early with engine and turret trouble. Of the remainder one attacked Swinemunde and one Bremen and the remaining 5 attacked the target; fires were seen. One aircraft badly damaged by flak and then attacked by a night fighter wounding the second Pilot Sgt. Masse and the rear gunner Sgt. Pullen, but made a successful crash landing at base.

One aircraft brushed a tree landing, owing to wrong altimeter setting.

14th-15th August, 1941

Magdeburgh. 7 aircraft. 2 brought their bombs back as they could not find the target. Of the remainder, 3 attacked the target, 2 Hannover and one Rotterdam, owing to a late start.

One aircraft failed to return.

W 5496 (M)

P/O Fleming Killed.
Sgt. Lesley Killed.
Sgt. Dawson Killed.
Sgt. Stott Killed.
Sgt. Stansfield Killed.
Sgt. Malloy Killed.

At 00.30 hours the airfield was attacked by an enemy aircraft which dropped incendiaries around the Maintenance Hangar and high explosives on fields around the airfield. Apart from slight damage to one aircraft, this attack was ineffective but a "Freshman" operation with 2 aircraft was cancelled.

16th-17th August, 1941

Cologne. 8 aircraft. One did not start. 6 bombed the target successfully but one aircraft was badly damaged by a night fighter and the rear gunner (Sgt. Payton) was killed. A fire which broke out in this aircraft was extinguished by the crew. The left wheel of this aircraft was punctured by flak but the aircraft landed safely.

One "Freshman" aircraft bombed Dusseldorf due to navigational error.

17th August, 1941

W/C Fenwick - Wilson A.F.C. took command of No 405 Squadron.

19th August, 1941

Funeral of Sgt. Payton killed on operations 16th-17th August, held at Barmby Moor.

19th-20th August, 1941

Kiel. 6 aircraft. One brought bombs back as it was unable to find the target. The remainder were forced to bomb on E.T.A. through thick cloud.

22nd August, 1941

Two aircraft overshot on landing due to 180 degree wind shift. One slightly damaged and one badly damaged, but only minor injuries to crew.

22nd-23rd August, 1941

Mannhelm/Ludwigshaven. 6 aircraft. Flak and searchlights moderate. Pink V observed flashed in morse near Cnarlroi. (This is the spelling in the Operations Record Book, but it could be Charlroi).

Le Havre. "Freshman" operation. Cancelled.

26th August, 1941

The airfield was attacked by enemy aircraft which dropped 8 high explosive bombs, damaging the runway and one aircraft which was about to take off on a "Freshman" operation. No casualties.

28th-29th August, 1941

Duisburg. 11 aircraft. 8 bombed the target and the attack appeared successful; large explosions and fires seen. One aircraft bombed Mundleheim after being caught and held by searchlights near Dusseldorf and one bombed the airfield at Haamsterne after being damaged by flak.

One aircraft did not return.

(D)

P/O Watts Killed.
Sgt. Quinn Prisoner of War.
Sgt. Hughes Killed.
Sgt. Davies Killed.
Sgt. Hollobone Killed.
Sgt. McLeod Prisoner of War.

1st September, 1941

One aircraft crash landed following engine fire but all the crew were unhurt.

3rd-4th September, 1941

Brest. 9 aircraft. Recalled owing to deteriorating weather.

7th-8th September, 1941

Berlin. 8 aircraft. Attack pressed home in good visibility despite strong opposition. One aircraft bombed Emden due to intercom trouble. One Aircraft failed to return.

(P)

Sgt. Saunders Prisoner of War.
Sgt. Macnutt Prisoner of War.
F/L MacKay Prisoner of War.
F/S Perkin Prisoner of War (Wounded).
Sgt. Courtnall Prisoner of War.
Sgt. Smith Prisoner of War.

Boulogne. One "Freshman" aircraft. Successful attack in spite of strong opposition.

10th-11th September, 1941

Turin. 5 aircraft. One did not start. This was the first attack on an Italian target and Stradishall was used as an advanced base. The bombing was affected by cloud and crews bombed on fires caused by earlier aircraft.

Results good so far as can be ascertained. Crews described the trip through the Alps as "lovely" with Mont Blanc standing out bright and clear. Flak negligible and very little searchlight activity.

12th-13th September, 1941

Frankfurt. 7 aircraft. One returned early, 5 bombed the target in very cloudy conditions and one Mainz, 20 miles away.

One aircraft damaged in a heavy landing at Alconbury in bad visibility.

15th-16th September, 1941

Hamburg. 7 aircraft. One did not start and one returned early with intercom and hydraulic trouble. 3 bombed the primary target causing much damage, one Wilhelmshaven with good results and one an intense flak concentration near Marne. Intense flak and searchlights. The aircraft which attacked Wilhelmshaven pressed on in spite of W.T. failure.

Hamburg. 2 "Freshman" also attacked this target.

18th September, 1941

Aircraft carrying out routine wireless test crashed at Northfield Farm, Barmby Moor, killing all 8 on board. Sgt.'s Chandos, Thompson, Turton, Phillips, Fletcher, Maxon, Struther and A.C. Armitage. This crash was apparently due to the dingy coming adrift and fouling the tail plane.

19th-20th September, 1941

Stettin. 5 aircraft. 3 bombed the target and saw enormous fires. One bombed Rotterdam after intercom failure and one a flak concentration near Flensburg.

One aircraft did not return after giving "off target" signal.

(F)

Sgt. Dougall Prisoner of War.
P/O Towler Prisoner of War.
Sgt. Lord Prisoner of War.
Sgt. Clayden Prisoner of War (Died in captivity).
Sgt. Emsley Prisoner of War.
Sgt. Foreman Prisoner of War.

20th-21st September, 1941

Ostend. 3 "Freshmen" aircraft. Fires were seen. Two aircraft had near misses with balloons in the Harwich area, fortunately these were illuminated by searchlights.

22nd September, 1941

Funeral held at Barmby Moor of Sgt.'s Struther, Thompson, Turton and Maxon killed on the 18th September. Sgt. Maxon was an American from Galesburgh, Illonois. Mrs. V. Massey and Mr. Massey the Canadian High Commissioner and his wife visited the station.

29th-30th September, 1941

Stettin. 6 aircraft. 5 attacked the target and one a town near Stettin probably Stolzenburg. Good results obtained in cloudless weather. 2 aircraft fired on by a convoy near Skipsea.

Hamburg. 2 "Freshmen" aircraft. Successful operation.

30th September - 1st October, 1941

Hamburg. 3 aircraft. All claimed to have bombed the primary target. 2 aircraft carried cameras for the first time. One showed only fields but the other a good photo of the Blohm und Voss Shipyards.

1st October, 1941

Construction of new East/West Runway started.

3rd October, 1941

One aircraft damaged when it overshot the runway. This aircraft was clearing the runway for another aircraft and went through the hedge due to low brake pressure. Pilots first solo on Wellington II.

3rd-4th October, 1941

Dunkirk. 1 "Freshman" aircraft. Returned early due to engine trouble.

6th October, 1941

Station Dental Centre opened.

10th-11th October, 1941

Essen. 5 aircraft. There were a number of "hang-ups" due to faulty bomb gear and icing. All aircraft reached the target, cloud and haze hampered this operation but some fires were seen. Defences moderate.

Ostend. 5 "Freshmen" aircraft. Three were successful but 2 became lost due to haze and jettisoned.

12th-13th October, 1941

Nuremburg. 7 aircraft. One had a taxiing accident when it hit a fence. 2 did not start, one returned early with engine trouble and one was forced to land at Swanton Morley also with engine trouble. The remaining 2 claimed to have bombed the target, however only a few bombs fell on Nuremburg on this night, the majority falling on Layingen 65 miles away and Lauffen 95 miles away.

One aircraft returned from the target on one engine. Several aircraft diverted to Pocklington due to bad weather.

14th-15th October, 1941

Nuremburg. 5 aircraft. One became bogged at dispersal and one did not start. The remaining 3 did not claim to have bombed the target after a very bad trip with icing and static. There was a snowstorm over the target and aircraft were only able to bomb fires. One aircraft hit by flak over Darnstat. All aircraft returned to Horsham St. Faith.

Halifax's at dispersal point as darkness falls, ready for operation.
IWM Copyright

16th-17th October, 1941

Duisburg. 7 aircraft. 2 did not start and one returned early with rev counter unserviceable. 10/10 cloud. 4 bombed a flak concentration near the target and one Gilzerijen airfield which caused the flarepath to be doused. One aircraft almost collided head on with an ME 110, missing it only by about 8 ft.

17th October, 1941

One aircraft slightly damaged when it taxied into a fence.

19th October, 1941

Station Church dedicated by the Bishop of Selby. (This site now occupied by John Wetherill Electronics).

20th-21st October, 1941

Wilhelmshaven. 5 aircraft. One did not start and one returned early with pilot's mike unserviceable and parachute spilled. The remainder claimed to have bombed in the vicinity of the target. Flak intensive and fairly accurate.

Emden. 2 "Freshmen" aircraft. One did not start. The other bombed the target but, as with the Wilhemlshaven operation, haze did not allow results to be seen.

22nd-23rd October, 1941

Mannheim. 6 aircraft. (This operation was carried out from Linton on Ouse, due to NE/SW runway being unserviceable). One returned early due to excessive icing, putting turret unserviceable. One was forced to belly land clear of the runway at Linton due to engine failure.

The remaining aircraft were forced to bomb on E.T.A. through unbroken cloud.

Le Havre. One "Freshman" aircraft. Gave "off target" signal, but did not return.

(V)

Sgt. Hall Killed.   F/S Jackson Killed
Sgt. Walker Killed.   F/S Marr Killed.
Sgt. Johnstone Killed.
Sgt. Dodge Killed.

24th October, 1941

One airman was returned under Civil Police escort having been found guilty of 2 charges of common assault. Charged with:-

1. Being absent without leave.
2. Conduct prejuditial to discipline and good order. Found guilty at Court Martial and sentenced to 6 months detention.

24th-25th October, 1941

Frankfurt. 6 aircraft. One did not start. Only 2 reached the target but no results seen. One aircraft was hit by flak turned back and bombed Schowen airfield. A petrol leak caused this aircraft to catch fire on return. The aircraft was written off but all the crew escaped.

The remaining 2 aircraft bombed Ostend and Aachen.

31st October - 1st November, 1941

Hamburg. 9 aircraft. One returned early with intercom trouble. 4 saw the target and bombed through thick cloud but no results seen. The remainder attacked a flak concentration near Wilhelmshaven.

Dunkirk. 3 "Freshmen" aircraft. One was forced to jettison due to the de-icers being unserviceable but the remaining 2 carried out a successful attack.

Flak was not severe until after the raid started.

1st November, 1941

G/C W.A.D. Brook posted in as Station Commander.

G/C S.O. Bufton posted to Air Ministry and became Deputy Director of Bombing Operations and had a considerable part in the formation of the Pathfinders. After a distinguished career he retired from the R.A.F. with the rank of Air Vice Marshal, his final post being Deputy Chief of Air Vice (Intelligence).

4th-5th November, 1941

Dunkirk. 5 "Freshmen" aircraft. 2 found the target in spite of 10/10 cloud but the remaining 3 were forced to jettison. Flak accurate.

7th-8th November, 1941

Berlin. 10 aircraft. 6 aircraft attacked the target the remainder Kiel and Wilhelmshaven. Due to late take-off, all aircraft returned in daylight the last one landing as late as 08.20. There was 9/10 cloud all the way and some aircraft spent a considerable time over the target returning with little fuel, several were diverted to Binbrook and Docking. One aircraft crash landed at base on return. This was the last major raid on Berlin until January 1943.

One aircraft failed to return.

(D)

F/S Hassan Killed.
P/O Solheim Killed.
Sgt. Killin Killed.
Sgt. Hynam Killed.
F/S Bell Killed.
Sgt. McCleod Killed.

Boulogne. 2 "Freshmen" aircraft. Successful operation in spite of heavy flak and searchlight concentration. On return one aircraft nearly collided with the Dover Balloon Barrage.

9th-10th November, 1941

Hamburg. 4 aircraft. 3 attacked the target and one Wilhelmshaven. On return this aircraft was diverted to Linton on Ouse and landed with one wheel off the runway. This caused a violent swing and one engine caught fire in the subsequent ground loop. There were again fortunately no casualties. Searchlights numerous. Flak intense and accurate.

14th November, 1941

The satellite airfield at Melbourne was occupied by No 810 (Defence) Squadron.

15th-16th November, 1941

Emden. 2 "Freshmen" aircraft. This operation was carried out in thick cloud. One aircraft pin pointed Berkum and bombed on E.T.A. The other pin pointed Termunden and bombed West of the target. Opposition negligible.

30th November, 1941

Hamburg. 6 aircraft. 5 managed to identify and bomb the target.

One aircraft failed to return. Gave "Ops. Abandoned" signal but nothing further heard; aircraft presumed to have ditched but nothing found in spite of intense sea search. Flak not as intense as usual.

W 5476 (H)

S/L Bisset Killed.
F/S Knight Killed.
P/O Mather Killed.
Sgt. Evans Killed.
F/S Hillmer Killed.
F/S Mann Killed.

Emden. 2 "Freshmen" aircraft. One bombed fires at Wesermunde and the other fires at Seestermunde due to faulty navigation.

Ostend. 1 "Freshman" aircraft. Turned back due to weather.

1st-2nd December, 1941

One aircraft damaged when it overshot landing in poor visibility with ineffective brakes.

7th-8th December, 1941

Dunkirk. 2 "Freshmen" aircraft. Both were unable to find the target in 10/10 cloud so jettisoned and returned.

13th December, 1941

Further aircraft badly damaged, landing in bad visibility.

15th December, 1941

Bad visibility and landing into low sun caused undercarriage of aircraft to collapse and aircraft swung off runway.

15th-16th December, 1941

Ostend. 2 "Freshmen" aircraft. One bombed successfully but the other was unable to identify the target so jettisoned and returned.

16th-17th December, 1941

Wilhelmshaven. 9 aircraft. One was forced to jettison and return due to frozen up A.S.I. One bombed Bremen starting a large fire and the remainder successfully attacked the target including one which made the whole trip on astro as W.T. was U/S. However, little damage was done on this raid.

2 parachutes were seen only 100 yards from one aircraft.

Dunkirk. One "Freshman" aircraft. Successful operation. Large fire started.

17th-18th December, 1941

Le Havre. 3 "Freshmen" aircraft. One managed to bomb in spite of 10/10 cloud but the other 2 were forced to jettison. One aircraft had to divert to Balderton on return.

22nd-23rd December, 1941

Wilmhelmshaven. 12 aircraft. 2 did not start and one returned early due to icing. A second aircraft abandoned this operation and crashed at Lindholme after the port engine failed on the way out, with only slight casualties to the crew.

The remainder attacked the target with the exception of one who bombed the seaplane base at Borkum.

27th-28th December, 1941

Boulogne. 2 "Freshmen" aircraft. Both attacked successfully but one had to divert to Hibaldstow on return.

Emden. 5 aircraft. Perfect weather and snow showing up features well. All aircraft bombed the target and also started fires at Wilhelmshaven.

One aircraft did not return.

(J)

Sgt. Williams Killed.
Sgt. Gordon Killed.
F/S Donkin Killed.
Sgt. James Killed.
Sgt. Langhorne Killed.
F/S Borgeau Killed.

Church at Barmby near Pocklington. (war graves to right of church)

9/10 March 1942. All aircraft returned safely to pocklington, except one which landed at Squaires Gate Airfield, Blackpool.
(Navigator - This doesn't look like Pocklington Tower Skip)

Thank God We Ran Out of Petrol Before We Ran Out Of Land.

cartoon by F/O John J. Jamieson DFM.

In the early days of the War before the general use of Radar aids, navigation at night was very difficult. Particularly if a fault developed in the navigation instruments.

1942

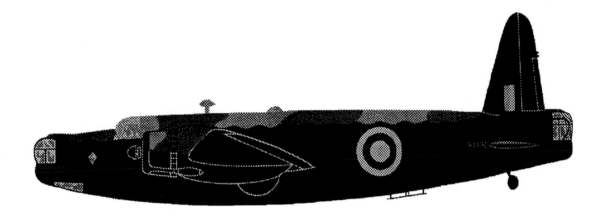

Eastward they climb back shapes against the grey,
Of falling dusk, gone with the nodding day,
From English fields,
Not theirs the sudden glow
Of triumph that their fighter brothers know,
Only to fly through cloud, through storm, through night,
Unerring, and to keep their purpose bright,
Nor turn until their dreadful duty done,
Westward they climb to race the awakened sun.
Anon.

Following the attack on Russia on 22nd June, 1941 the air raids on the United Kingdom diminished but 1942 saw the commencement of the "Baedeker" raids on cities such as Exeter (bombed on 24th April), York, Bath and Norwich. The morale of the British people was however given a considerable uplift on the 30th May, when the first "Thousand Bomber" raid was launched against Cologne. To many people this was the turning point of the War.

So far as the other countries were concerned, the Americans had entered the War following the attack in Pearl Harbour on December 7th 1941 and the slow build up of both the American Army and the Eighth Air Force in the United Kingdom command that it would be 1943 before they were in a position to attack Germany.

North Africa saw the advance of Rommel's forces to El Alamein in July but an attack by the Eighth Army on October 24th saw the start of the defeat of the Germans in North Africa.

On the Eastern Front the Germans had advanced as far as Stalingrad and in the Far East the Japanese had advanced as far as the Burma/Indian Border. Singapore had fallen and the Japanese had occupied Malaya.

5th January 1942

Aircraft (W 5589) on routine air test crashed attempting to force land at Strensall, north of York when one engine caught fire. All 5 on board killed Sgt. Wityck, Sgt. Garrow, Sgt. Robertson and Sgt. Gayfer were killed.

The weather was very bad at the time. The wireless operator of this aircraft, Sgt. Robson missed the transport and was not on board.

6th-7th January 1942

Cherbourg. 5 "Freshman" Aircraft. 2 bombed the target but the remainder forced to jettison in 10/10 cloud. Small amount of intense heavy flak.

On return one aircraft landed at Holme-on-Spalding Moor. This aircraft had been cleared to land at Pocklington by R.T. but was in fact in the Holme-on-Spalding Moor circuit. A "Red" was given too late and this aircraft collided with an unlit No 458 Squadron aircraft. No casualties but both aircraft were written off.

7th January 1942

Aircraft badly damaged when it failed to take off due to ice and frost on wings.

7th-8th January 1942

St. Nazaire. 5 aircraft. One brought bombs back due to electrical failure. The rest bombed the target, the rear gunner of one aircraft shooting up the docks after the aircraft had bombed in a glide from 5000 ft.

8th January 1942

Crew of aircraft which crashed on the 5th January, Sgt.'s Lefurgy, Wityck, Garrow, Robertson and Gayfer buried at Barnby Moor. Photographs were taken and sent to their relatives.

15th-16th January, 1942

Emden. 4 "Freshmen" aircraft. One did not start. The remainder attacked the target and a large fire was seen. All aircraft diverted on return to Linton, Dalton, and Acklington.

17th-18th January, 1942

Bremen. 8 aircraft. 4 attacked the target and the rest the alternate (Emden). One aircraft dropped a 4000 lb bomb in the middle of Emden with "terrific" results.

One aircraft did not return. Flown by S/L Keddy, "The popular and able B Flight Commander", it ditched 20 miles from Skipsea.

(L)

S/L Keddy Killed.
Sgt. Masse Killed.
Sgt. Gale Killed.
F/S Carr Killed.
F/L Scrivens) Picked up by a destroyer after 17 hours in dinghy
Sgt. Turnbull) and taken to Sheppey County Hospital suffering badly from exposure.

21st January, 1942

Station visited by A.V.M. Edwards A.O.C. in Chief R.C.A.F. Overseas.

Station snow clearance operation used for the first time.

21st-22nd January, 1942

Bremen. 8 aircraft. 2 returned early due to engine trouble and brought their bombs back. 5 bombed the target with good results especially with 4000 lb bombs. One bombed Emden and one a flak concentration near Elsflethand. Ground was covered with snow and rivers frozen up. Flak reported as hectic and uncomfortably accurate.

24th January, 1942

One aircraft overshot on landing due to a combination of poor brakes and a wet runway.

26th January, 1942

The Q site (Decoy Airfield) at Burnby was brought into operation.

26th-27th January, 1942

Hannover. 9 aircraft. 2 did not start and 2 returned early. One with a failed engine and the other with its turrets unserviceable. 2 bombed the target and the remainder Brunswick and Bremen due to snow and frozen waterways making navigation difficult. One aircraft sighted 5 enemy aircraft in loose formation only 400 yards away, they did not attack. Photograph shows only fields.

One aircraft (S/L Fauquier) was fired on by a British Destroyer in spite of firing the correct colours. Pilot was reported as "Indignant."

28th-29th January, 1942

Boulogne. 3 "Freshmen" aircraft. One returned early. One was forced to jettison and one bombed Calais as there was 10/10 cloud over the target.

29th January, 1942

No 158 Squadron was detached from Driffield to Pocklington as their own airfield was unserviceable.

31st January - 1st February, 1942

Brest. 7 aircraft. 2 did not start. 3 bombed the target but the remainder brought their bombs back owing to smoke screen put out on arrival of first aircraft.

1st February, 1942

The Duke of Kent visited the Station, inspected crews and aircraft and stayed to lunch in the Officers Mess. The Duke of Kent was the principal R.A.F. Welfare Officer, a post in which he took a keen interest. He was killed in a Sunderland on August 25th, 1942 near Dunbeath in North Scotland.

6th February, 1942

Although weather fit for operations all aircraft were ordered to "Stand-by" from 3rd February, to the 8th February.

Refuelling from a 2,500 gallon tanker.
IWM Copyright

11th February, 1942

A.C. 2 Marriot. Seriously injured by propeller of aircraft when clearing snow. Died the following day in York Military Hospital.

11th-12th February, 1942

Le Havre. 2 "Freshmen" aircraft. One bombed the target but the other was unable to identify it and jettisoned.

Both aircraft reported bad "black-out" both in the target area and on route. Flak and searchlights were reported "sub-normal."

12th February, 1942

This was the day of the "Channel Dash" when the battleships Scharnhorst, Gneisenau and Prinz Eugen left Brest and sailed north up the Channel. The first wave of 6 aircraft from Pocklington saw nothing except one after searching at 300 ft.

The second wave consisted of 2 No 405 Squadron aircraft and one of No 158 Sqn. One jettisoned after a fruitless search, the other saw the ships through a momentary gap in the clouds and managed to straddle them but with no results. All aircraft received violent fire from warships.

One aircraft damaged landing at night. Pilot overshot due to instrument panel light not working and therefore not able to read A.S.I.

13th-14th February, 1942

Le Havre. 4 "Freshmen" aircraft. One carried leaflets as well as bombs and was successful but the remainder were unable to identify the target and jettisoned.

14th-15th February 1942

Mannheim. 6 aircraft. One did not start. No results observed owing to 10/10 cloud and in fact only slight damage was done. Two aircraft brought their bombs back owing to technical trouble. One aircraft of No 158 Squadron also took part but brought bombs back due to severe icing.

21st February 1942

W/C Fenwick-Wilson A.F.C. appointed Station Commander.

25th February 1942

Aircraft of No 158 Squadron hit a tree landing in bad visibility following an air test.

26th-27th February 1942

Kiel. 9 aircraft. Two brought their bombs back owing to weather. One jettisoned due to icing and an aircraft of No 158 Squadron crashed 1 1/2 miles north of Pocklington at Yapham. All the crew F/S Robb, Sgt. Hackney, Sgt Bennet, Sgt. Winterton, Sgt Morgan and F/S Brown were killed.

Four aircraft definitely bombed the target and one attacked Schleswig. The flak on this occasion was described as "tremendous". One aircraft failed to return.

(D)

F/L Robson Killed
W/C MacAllister Killed
Sgt. Dyson Killed
F/S Phillips Killed
F/S Piers Killed
F/S Robson Killed (F/S Robson was the survivor of the Strensall crash on 5th January)

27th February 1942

S/L Fauquier took command of No 405 Squadron. "Johnny" Fauquier became one of the most highly decorated Officers of World War II. A bush pilot before the war he had logged about 3000 hours before he joined up. Subsequent to commanding No 405 Squadron he served at R.C.A.F. Overseas Headquarters and with No 6 (R.C.A.F.) Bomber Group. He returned to command No 405 Squadron when they became the only R.C.A.F. Squadron in the Pathfinder Force. He was promoted to Air Commodore in 1944 but reverted to the rank of Group Captain and did a third tour commanding No 617 (Dambuster) Squadron, the only Dominion Officer to do so. He finished the war as an Air Commodore with two bars to his D.S.O. the D.F.C. the Croix de Guerre as well as being appointed a Chevalier of the Legion of Honour. He died in 1981 at the age of 72.

28th February 1942

Brigadier Eaker U.S.A.F. visited Pocklington.

One aircraft damaged when it burst a tyre on landing due to stones left on the runway on the runway by contractors. The undercarriage collapsed in the subsequent ground loop and one other aircraft burst a tyre landing in poor visibility.

The gymnasium in 1985

3rd March 1942

S/L Day gave a talk on German parachutists and other airbourne troops to defence and other officers. This talk was repeated on the 27th March.

3rd-4th March 1942

Paris (Renault Works) 10 aircraft of No 405 Squadron and 7 of No 158 Squadron. One did not start and 2 returned early one of which crashed north of Pocklington injuring three of the crew. This was a No 158 Squadron aircraft which was unable to feather the propeller after the engine failed. The other aircraft returned early due to engine trouble.

This was a successful raid but the weather was bad on return and all aircraft were diverted. One landed at East Wretham with undercarriage unserviceable but the crew were unhurt. This accident was due to the pilot retracting the undercarriage too early on take off.

This raid was biggest mounted by Bomber Command so far and the Renault Factory was hit by over 300 bombs. Sadly casualties to French civillians were high; 361 killed and 341 badly injured. A prominent citizen at Billancourt (where the factory was situated) M. Corse who was serving with the Free French in London wrote "those who have died also bought their own contribution to the coming of dawn." Presumably the people of Billancourt agreed as they elected M. Corse Mayor after the war.

4th March 1942

No 158 Squadron returned to Driffield.

5th March 1942

Film show held for defence personnel on the invasion of France and the Low Countries.

7th March 1942

The equipping of the gymnasium was completed (This building is at present occupied by John Wetherill Ltd Electronics). It also served as the Station Church.

7th-8th March 1942

St. Nazaire. 4 aircraft. One landed early at Middle Wallop due to fuel line trouble. The remaining three bombed the dock area and shipping. All aircraft diverted on return.

9th-10th March 1942

Essen. 7 aircraft. All claimed to have bombed the target but bombing was scattered over the whole Ruhr area. One aircraft collided with a balloon in the Ipswich area. All aircraft returned safely to Pocklington except one which landed at Squires Gate (Blackpool). Flak was reported as heavy and accurate. Three aircraft had minor damage.

10th-11th March 1942

Essen. 3 aircraft. One returned early with oil pressure trouble. Another disappointing raid. One aircraft failed to return. An S.O.S. was received from this aircraft (N) at 23.16 giving a position beyond the reach of rescue services so an International Broadcast was made. This was of no avail and the names of the crew, F/O Durbridge, F/S Lonergan, F/S Garnett, F/S Broddy, Sgt. Wright and Sgt. Tilley can be found, together with 20,000 other airmen who have no known grave on the Runneymede Memorial to the Missing.

The Runneymede Memorial to the Missing.

11th March 1942

S/L Fauquier promoted to Wing Commander.
W/C Fenwick-Wilson posted to Washington.

13th March 1942

One aircraft slightly damaged when it taxied into a post. One landed with drift on and swerved off the runway.

13th-14th March, 1942

Cologne. 6 aircraft. One did not start. One returned early with turrets unserviceable. Crews reported they could distinguish streets and bridges under the light of flares. This raid involving a total of 135 aircraft is considered to be the first successful attack using "Gee" and caused considerable damage, despite heavy flak.

15th March, 1942

Station visited by a party of A.T.C. Cadets from Leeds.

17th March, 1942

7 aircraft despatched on a night cross-country exercise. 2 were damaged, one overshot as a result of not closing the throttles on time and the other landed heavily.

18th March, 1942

Brigadier Portman inspected the Station Defence Scheme and reported it as "Most Satisfactory."

19th March, 1942

Practice night air raid warning held.

21st March, 1942

Station provided personnel for the Pocklington Town Warship Week and also staged Boxing and Rugby matches. Station land cultivation scheme put into operation.

22nd March, 1942

S/L Harston, Chaplain in Chief R.C.A.F., preached at Station Church. Parachute demonstration took place at Market Weighton. Local civilian defence exercise held.

One aircraft landed heavily, bursting a tyre and collapsing undercarriage.

25th-26th March, 1942

Essen. 7 aircraft. One did not start and 2 returned early. One of which became lost over Holland and brought its bombs back and the other being unable to climb so bombed the flare path at Remanuel. The remaining 4 bombed the Rhur area in very bad weather.

Many bombs on this raid were drawn off by a decoy fire at Rheinburg.

26th-27th March, 1942

Essen. 5 aircraft. All claimed to have bombed successfully but again only a few bombs fell on Essen. One aircraft hit by flak putting both turrets unserviceable but flak generally was moderate and inaccurate.

27th March, 1942

One aircraft burst a tyre landing heavily. Aircraft swung violently and undercarriage collapsed.

28th-29th March, 1942

Lubeck. 9 aircraft. 2 returned early, one with intercom failure and the other with an unserviceable compass and landed at Drem. 5 aircraft carried incendiaries and 4 x 4000 lb bombs. The remaining 7 aircraft attacked the target, some as low as 2000 ft. and leaving fires which were still visible from 100 miles on the way home. Both heavy and light flak was inaccurate. Few fighters seen. One aircraft attacked by an ME 110 but lost it after evasive action. Few searchlights.

This raid was a major success. 30% of the built up area was destroyed together with the highest number of fatal casualties (about 320) on a German city so far.

It was later agreed via the International Red Cross not to bomb Lubeck again as this port was used for the shipping of Red Cross Supplies.

31st March, 1942

The station F.A. Team unbeaten this season reached the semi-final of the York District Cup.

L.A.C. N.R. McLeod of Ontario died in York Military Hospital after a short illness.

During the month of March, a scheme was brought into use to train ground staff in the use of small arms for anti-invasion purposes. This included route marches, P.T. and instruction in the use of machine guns, rifles and pistols and also grenade throwing and tactics.

1st April, 1942

W.A.A.F. Quarters at Allerthorpe opened. 100 W.A.A.F.'s arrived to work in H.Q. Accounts, Equipment, Messes and M.T.

1st-2nd April, 1942

Poissy nr. Paris (Ford Motor Works). 4 aircraft. This attack was at first thought to be successful but this was not confirmed by later photo reconnaissance. Flak slight but moderate.

One aircraft did not return.

F/S Howsan Killed.
F/S Howe Killed.
P/O Burgoyne Prisoner of War.
Sgt. Page Killed.
Sgt. Ashun Killed.
P/O McKinnon Killed.

Le Havre. 5 "Freshmen" aircraft. All bombed successfully except one which dropped bombs safe. Flak moderate and inaccurate.

4th April, 1942

S/L McCormack, B Flight Commander and F/L Featherstone, the Senior Navigation Officer, were killed when the station Magister crashed near Barmby Moor in the afternoon. S/L McCormack had completed 25 operations.

This aircraft failed to complete a slow roll at a low altitude and dived vertically into the ground. As a result of this accident an order was made restricting operational pilots to their own Squadron type.

5th-6th April, 1942

Cologne. 7 aircraft. One did not start due to taxiing accident. Weather fairly good, all aircraft claimed to have bombed the target in spite of fairly intense heavy and light flak. Some fires seen but the attack had no great weight. One aircraft produced a good target photograph of Bonn.

Le Havre. 2 "Freshmen" aircraft. One did not start. The other bombed successfully.

6th-7th April, 1942

Essen. 4 aircraft. 2 turned back due to weather. The remainder bombed on E.T.A. One aircraft (P/0 Allison) was coned by searchlights over Brussels for 3-4 minutes and engaged by flak. This occurred again over Erkelenz. Over Eindhoven chased by JU 88 and shook it off after violent evasive action. Flak over the target was light but increased as raid progressed.

A "Freshman" operation to Brussels with 4 aircraft with Nickels (Leaflets) was cancelled due to weather.

8th April, 1942

Funeral of S/L McCormack and F/L Featherstone held at Barmby Moor. Photographs taken which will be sent to their relatives.

8th-9th April, 1942

Hamburg. 8 aircraft. One returned early with magneto trouble in the port engine. 4 aircraft believed they had bombed the target in very bad weather. The rest bombed Wilhelmshaven, Bremen and Wessermunder.

One aircraft failed to return. It was given a Q.D.M. at 03.46 and transmitted an S.O.S. at 04.00 followed by a message "landing on beach." Key jammed and a further Q.D.M. given. Nothing further heard. Sea search fruitless.

(B)

P/O Locke Killed.
Sgt. Edwards Killed.
F/S Lefty Killed.
Sgt. Jones Killed.
Sgt. Dennis Killed.
F/S Sanderson Killed.

Brussels. One "Freshman" aircraft dropped leaflets. No opposition.

9th April, 1942

2 aircraft in sea search for aircraft missing from previous nights operations. Nothing found.

10th April, 1942

Station Commander's Quarter completed. (This building was used as the Wolds Gliding Club Clubhouse for some years. It has since been demolished).

One aircraft damaged when the tail lifted as the engines were being run up.

10th-11th April, 1942

Essen. 3 aircraft. 2 bombed on E.T.A. and one through lucky break in cloud. Heavy flak, numerous searchlights. Many enemy aircraft sighted but no attacks.

Le Havre. 3 "Freshmen" aircraft. One returned early as I.F.F. was unserviceable. One bombed successfully and one was forced to jettison following evasive action.

11th April, 1942

F/L Kingsley arrived with a collection of German Air Force and other relics.

12th-13th April, 1942

Essen. 7 aircraft. Owing to a series of technical failures only 2 aircraft bombed the target and once again the results were not compatable with the 251 aircraft engaged in this operation. On return one aircraft was fired at by a convoy damaging perspex and tyres.

One aircraft, captained by F/S Lloyd had engine trouble on the way to the target. 4 of the crew baled out successfully but F/S Graves was unable to find his parachute. F/S Lloyd "who sacrificed his life in an action of conspicuous gallantry" then attempted to force land but the aircraft crashed at Greeting St Mary killing both occupants.

Le Havre. 2 "Freshmen" aircraft. Both believed they had bombed the dock area. Only slight flak.

13th April, 1942

A.O.C. 4 Group visited Pocklington.

14th April, 1942

Works Department A.R.P. exercise held.

14th-15th April, 1942

Dortmund. 6 aircraft. One returned early with intercom trouble, radio and generator out of action. This raid was scattered over a 40 mile stretch of the Ruhr.

On return one crew was forced to bale out between Winchester and Basingstoke owing to fuel shortage. Most of the crew landed near Petersfield.

2 aircraft failed to return one of which, put out a distress signal over Cherbourg; as this was out of the reach of the rescue services an International Broadcast was made. The crew were all picked up.

Increased heavy flak at coast but only slight at target.

(X)
F/L Toft Prisoner of War.
P/O Samson Prisoner of War.
F/S Bydwell Prisoner of War.
W/O Crowe Prisoner of War.
Sgt. Hesseldon Prisoner of War.

(N)
Sgt. MacFarlane Killed.
Sgt. Harvey Killed.
Sgt. Jones Killed.
F/S Cormack Killed.
P/O Tuck Killed.

15th April, 1942

Pocklington F.A. Team beaten by R.A.F. Linton on Ouse in the Semi-Final of the York District Cup.

15th-16th April, 1942

Dortmund. 4 aircraft. Due to 10/10 cloud all aircraft forced to bomb on E.T.A. No results seen.

16th April, 1942

Lecture given by Commander Newman R.N. on "Convoys."

17th April, 1942

Sgts. Mess Dance held. All W.A.A.F.'s invited. (B & C Motors now occupy the site of the Sgts. Mess).

The Sergeants Mess in 1985

17th-18th April, 1942

Hamburg. 7 aircraft. 2 did not start and one returned early with rev. counter unserviceable. Due to thick weather only one aircraft bombed the target. The remainder attacked Cuxhaven, Kiel, and the Isle of Bactrum. Heavy flak over Hamburg and at the coast.

This was the last Wellington Operation of No 405 Squadron. To mark the occasion a number of empty beer bottles were dropped on searchlights at Wesermunde and Cuxhaven with inconclusive results.

By a somewhat odd coincidence, 60,000 bottles of alcohol were destroyed in the warehouse of a drinks manufacturer in Hamburg on this night.

18th April, 1942

4 aircraft in a sea search for missing Driffield aircraft. Nothing found.

Funeral of F/S Lloyd and F/S Graves held at Wattisham.

23rd April, 1942

5 Halifax aircraft arrived from Middleton St George. One crashed on landing. Crew unhurt.

25th April, 1942

No 405 Squadron held a party in the Regent Palace Hotel, London.

2 Halifax II aircraft arrived from Croft.

26th April, 1942

One Operational Halifax II aircraft arrived from Ringway.

29th April, 1942

A number of German aircraft which had attacked York flew low over Pocklington. Flares were dropped but there was no attack.

The body of the pilot of a crashed German aircraft (JU 88) Leutenant Werner Boy brought to Pocklington from Escrick.

30th April, 1942

Princess Royal visited Pocklington and opened Y.M.C.A. Tea Bar.

Funeral of Sgt. Edwards missing since the 9th April, held at Catfoss. Sgt. Edwards body was recovered from the sea on the 25th April, 1942.

During the month of April a considerable area of the Station was planted with potatoes and other vegetables and the look of the Station was improved by the planting of trees and shrubs.

2nd May, 1942

Funeral of Leutenant Werner Boy held at Barmby Moor. He was buried with full military honours. His body was exhumed after the War and taken to Germany.

One Halifax II aircraft arrived from Preston.

6th May, 1942

Heath fire at Allerthorpe Common. Though this was 3/4 of a mile from dispersal all aircraft in the vicinity were moved as a precaution.

7th May, 1942

A series of social evenings begun in W.A.A.F.'s Quarters at Allerthorpe.

11th May, 1942

Manning exercise held to practice defence of aircraft dispersals.

13th May, 1942

Body of S/L Keddy missing since 17th January, washed up at Hornsea. Body taken to Catfoss.

14th May, 1942

Practice anti-invasion exercise held. Strong complaint of shortage of rifles. Only 900 for 2000 men.

Captured German aircraft arrived a Heinkel III JU 88 and 2 ME 110's.

One aircraft slightly damaged in taxiing accident.

15th May, 1942

German aircraft demonstrated. G.C. Brook flew as passenger in ME 110.

16th May, 1942

G.C. W.A.D. Brook posted to 4 Group H.Q.

G.C. E.C. Corbally posted from Middleton St George as Station Commander.

19th May, 1942

Funeral of S/L Keddy held at Hull Crematorium. His ashes were later scattered in the sea from a Pocklington Wellington.

Hostile aircraft reported in the area. One bomb was dropped at Fangfoss but the only casualties were cattle.

Anti-invasion exercise held. Successful but there was considerable lack of arms for R.A.F. Personnel.

20th May, 1942

Air raid warning. One bomb dropped 3-4 miles from airfield.

25th May, 1942

All personnel recalled from leave as No 405 Squadron now ready for operations 16 crews and 14 aircraft operationally fit.

Corporals held a dance. Station band in attendance.

26th May, 1942

A.O.C. No 4 Group visited Pocklington and addressed crews. "Too many crews were bombing dummy fires. Don't bomb an existing fire. Start one of your own."

27th May, 1942

Armament section worked late into the night to belt 100,000 rounds of ammunition for Halifax Aircraft.

30th-31st May, 1942

Cologne. 19 aircraft. (Including 3 from the conversion flight). 5 did not start, one returned early due to icing. This was the first "Thousand Bomber" raid and consisted of 131 Halifax's, 602 Wellingtons, 88 Stirlings, 79 Hampdens, 73 Lancasters, 46 Manchesters and 78 Whitleys. The target was reported to be a mass of flames with defences reduced to impotence.

One aircraft was attacked by an ME 110 which hit the tail plane.

The aircraft which returned early blocked the runway and 4 aircraft landed at Melbourne which was used for the first time.

One aircraft failed to return.

Sgt. Wadman Killed.
Sgt. Acton Killed.
F/S Welsh Killed.
Sgt. Pickett Killed.
Sgt. McClean Killed.
Sgt. Henning Killed.
P/O Sankey Killed.

31st May, 1942

Bombing operation with 14 aircraft cancelled.

By the end of the month the fourth runway, 10 blast shelters and the extensions to the W.A.A.F. Quarters at Allerthorpe were completed.

1st-2nd June, 1942

Essen. (Krupps Works). 16 aircraft (including 3 from the conversion flight). This was the second "Thousand Bomber" raid but in fact 950 took part. The defences were reported to be light but owing to haze and low cloud bombing was scattered.

One aircraft failed to return.

W 7713 (T)

P/O Baltzer Killed.
Sgt. Turnbull Killed.
P/O Certy Killed.
F/S Jackson Killed.
F/S Reid Killed.
F/S Fortin Killed.
F/S Thompson Killed.

2nd-3rd June, 1942

Essen. 6 aircraft. One did not start. One returned early due to engine trouble and brought it's bombs back. One attacked by ME 110 and forced to jettison after violent evasive action. The remaining 3 reached the target but haze made observation of results difficult and the attack was widely scattered.

2 aircraft hit by flak.

3rd-4th June, 1942

Bremen. 7 aircraft. One did not start, one returned early due to shortage of fuel. Target was reported as obscured by haze and opposition moderate. Later however, this was found to have been a heavy accurate attack doing considerable damage.

4th June, 1942

Message from A.O.C. Bomber Command (Air Vice Marshal Harris) thanking all concerned with the "Thousand Bomber raids" "Climax of months of patience and cunning contrivance."

6th-7th June, 1942

Emden. 14 aircraft. One did not start and one returned early due to engine trouble after getting within 30 miles of the target. Target attacked against "moderate" defences. Later photographs showed considerable damage.

The mighty Halifax set against the setting sun
IWM copyright

One aircraft crashed near Binbrook with both outer engines on fire. The crew all baled out successfully.

8th-9th June, 1942

Essen. 11 aircraft. One did not start. One returned early when the starboard inner engine cut out. One could not find the target so bombed unidentified area as time limit of attack had expired. Terrific opposition and raid widely scattered owing to ground haze and searchlight glare.

3 aircraft did not return.

(D)
F/S Fleming Killed.
F/S Platt Killed.
Sgt. Holland Killed.
Sgt. Jackson Killed.
F/S Montgomery Killed.
F/S Cattle Killed.
P/O Morris Killed

(U)
P/O Higginson Killed.
Sgt. Riches Prisoner of War.
P/O McEwan Killed.
F/S McGill Killed.
F/S Haycock Killed.
F/S Jeffries Killed.
F/S Healey Killed.
Sgt. Pethybridge Killed.

(H)
F/L McClean evaded capture & returned to U.K.
Sgt. Shields Prisoner of War.
P/O Warnham Prisoner of War.
Sgt. Kerr Prisoner of War.
F/S Potter Prisoner of War.
F/S Olsen Prisoner of War.
Sgt. Forbes Prisoner of War.
(F/L McClean was to have a distinguished career in Canadian Politics after the War).

13th June, 1942

Film "Next of Kin" shown to all personnel. Repeated next day.

16th-17th June, 1942

Essen or Bonn. 8 aircraft. One returned early due to icing. One attacked Essen and 6 Bonn encountering very accurate predicted flak, estimated at about 100 guns. No results observed owing to weather and both attacks scattered.

19th-20th June, 1942

Emden or Osnabruck. 7 aircraft. Crews ordered to bomb on flares. 5 attacked Emden, one Osnabruck and one an unidentified area East of Emden. Both attacks met heavy and light flak of moderate intensity and very little damage was done to either target.

20th June, 1942

F/L Durnford lectured aircrew on escape of P.O.W.'s in enemy hands.

20th-21st June, 1942

Emden. 9 aircraft. All attacked target by "Navigational Aids" (presumably this is a reference to Gee and is the first mention of it in the Pocklington Operations Record Book). Oppostion moderate.

On return 6 aircraft from No 78 Squadron (Middleton St George) and one from No 10 Squadron (Leeming) were diverted to Pocklington.

22nd-23rd June, 1942

Emden. 10 aircraft. (This was the fourth attack on this target in a fortnight). Weather better and all aircraft bombed a well illuminated target except one who could not open the bomb doors and jettisoned on the way home. Considerable light flak. One aircraft attacked by a night fighter which wounded 2 of the crew and damaged the mid upper turret. However, a large decoy fire drew many bombs on this operation.

25th June, 1942

Sgt. James lectured aircrew on his escape from enemy territory.

25th-26th June, 1942

Bremen. 19 aircraft. (Including 2 from the Conversion Flight). 2 returned early one with rear and mid upper turrets unserviceable and the other could not maintain height or speed. This was to have been the third "Thousand Bomber" raid but in fact only 960 were despatched. Unbroken cloud over the target forced crews to bomb blind on the glow of fires. 2 bombed the alternative Wilhelmshaven and F/S Barton braved the defences of Hamburg almost in daylight. "His trip resulted in considerable expenditure of German ammunition and wasted many man hours of Hamburg's vast industries irrespective of the damage caused and many Germans must have had their nights sleep disturbed."

27th-28th June, 1942

Bremen. 11 aircraft. One returned early due to icing. Bombed on glow of fires through cloud. Moderate heavy and intense light flak. Several night fighters seen but only one combat with the aircraft flown by F/S Barton. He was attacked by 2 enemy fighters. Violent evasive action put aircraft on it's back and 5 000 ft. were lost before recovery could be effective.

Two aircraft failed to return.

(C)	(Q)
W/O Scott Killed.	F/S Field Killed.
Sgt. Tatham Killed.	Sgt. Ansell Killed.
F/S Phillips Killed.	F/S Fitzgerald Killed.
Sgt. Hughes Killed.	Sgt. Smith Killed.
F/S Cole Killed.	Sgt. Danby Killed.
F/S Lacelle Killed.	F/S Ailey Killed.
Sgt. Rowland Killed.	Sgt. Kleisdorf Killed.

29th June, 1942

W.A.A.F.'s held a Birthday Party in their Quarters.

29th-30th June, 1942

Bremen. 9 aircraft. One returned early with rear turret guns unserviceable and one jettisoned near Oldenburg due to engine trouble. Bombed on "Navigational Aids" dead reckoning and E.T.A. Photographs showed fires but no ground detail. Moderate to intense heavy and light flak.

3 aircraft failed to return.

(H)	(G)
F/L Liversidge Killed.	F/S Chinn Killed.
Sgt. Bradbrook Killed.	Sgt. Harrell Killed.
Sgt. Alcazar Killed.	Sgt. Simpson Killed.
Sgt. Dearlove Killed.	F/S Bell Killed.
Sgt. Foot Killed.	F/S Oneson Killed.
Sgt. Dumond Prisoner of War.	Sgt. Dickinson Killed.
(Wounded).	F/S Adams Killed.
Sgt. McFee Killed.	Sgt. Bears Killed.

(K)
F/S Sidney Killed.
Sgt. Walsh Killed.
Sgt. Brennan Killed.
F/S Gorieu Killed.
Sgt. Gunn Killed.
F/S Philp Killed.
Sgt. White Killed.

W/C Fauquier was engaged by 2 light guns and 2 searchlights. Came down to 100 ft. when his gunners knocked out one gun and one searchlight.

1st July, 1942

Canadian Dominion Day. Highly successful sports meeting held.

Dance held in the Officers Mess. A Cafe now stands on this site on the north side of the A 1079 opposite the Lane to Allerthorpe. (Unoccupied at present)

2nd-3rd July, 1942

Bremen. 11 aircraft. One did not start. 8 reached the target, but could not pinpoint owing to haze however a large fire was seen in the dock area. One aircraft (S/L Fraser) had a close flak burst under right wing which turned aircraft on its back. The aircraft then "flick rolled" during recovery after which the elevator trim was found to be U/S. This aircraft bombed Ardorf Airfield with no visible results and another aircraft which had intercom failure bombed searchlights and flak at Ameland Island. Moderate heavy and some light flak. Numerous searchlights and many dummy fires seen.

3rd July, 1942

One aircraft on sea search. Nothing found.

4th July, 1942

Corporal court martialled for stealing rations. Reduced to ranks and given 56 days detention.

6th July, 1942

Funeral of F/S Lefty lost in the 9th April held at Great Bircham "In quaint Bircham Newton Cemetery with full military honours. It was a sunny day and pictures were taken which will be forwarded to his parents."

8th July, 1942

One aircraft slightly damaged when it taxied into engine stand.

8th-9th July, 1942

Wilhelmshaven. 9 aircraft. All bombed the target except one which overshot due to electrical failure. Several fires observed which increased in intensity as aircraft left. Opposition not very intense. Later photographs showed most of the bombing fell to the west of the target in open country. However, some damage was done.

10th July, 1942

Bishop Nelligan, Principal Roman Catholic Chaplain, Canadian Forces visited Pocklington.

12th July, 1942

One aircraft crashed at Aberporth (North Wales) when attempting a forced landing following engine failure.

One crew member slightly injured.

13th-14th July, 1942

Duisburg. 8 aircraft. One returned early due to lightning strike. The rest bombed in varying conditions and few results were observed. Bombing well scattered. Opposition less than usual.

2 aircraft were also detailed to drop leaflets in the Lyons area. This necessitated flying 1,300 miles in limited darkness.

14th July, 1942

A.O.C. R.C.A.F. Air Marshal Edwards visited Pocklington.

18th July, 1942

Station visited by party of A.T.C. Cadets from Morley area of Leeds for a weeks camp.

19th-20th July, 1942

Vegesack (Submarine Works and Naval Yards). 12 aircraft. One did not start and one returned early with unserviceable turret. Considerable heavy flak on the way to the target where there was moderate heavy and some light flak. Dummies and decoys also seen. The target which was completely cloud covered forcing aircraft to bomb on "Gee". No bombs fell on the target but some damage was done at Bremen a few miles away.

Weather bad on return and aircraft diverted to Eastmoor, Elvington and Linton.

20th July, 1942

Pocklington placed fourth in group gardening competition. 10 acres at Pocklington and 5 at Melbourne under cultivation providing fresh vegetables for Messes.

23rd-24th July, 1942

Duisburg. 9 aircraft. One returned early with intercom trouble. The weather for this operation was bad but 7 aircraft claimed to have bombed the target. Moderate heavy and some light flak. Many searchlights.

This operation was marred by the crash of "K" in New Street, Pocklington. The aircraft burnt out and all the crew, F/S Thurlow, Sgt. Apperson, F/S Hexter, Sgt. Owens, Sgt. Western, Sgt. Colloton, F/S Albright and P/O Strong were killed. Though the aircraft crashed in a very narrow part of the street, almost opposite the school, there were no casualties to civilians and only minor damage to one house.

2 minutes after this crash another aircraft whose pilot had been distracted by the burning wreck of "K" landed "Wheels Up".

25th-26th July, 1942

Duisburg. 8 aircraft. 2 returned early one with severe icing and the other with both turrets unserviceable. The visibility over the target was poor and no results observed. Later German news broadcast admitted damage done.

26th-27th July, 1942

Hamburg. 14 aircraft. One did not start. One returned early with port outer engine unserviceable.

This was a very effective attack doing considerable damage. Visibility over the target was excellent. Large fires were seen and opposition less than anticipated.

The S.A.S.O. 4 Group G/C Brook flew on this operation as P2 to W/C Fauquier.

One aircraft held by searchlights for an hour before being forced to jettison.
2 aircraft failed to return.

(L)	(P)
Sgt. Smith Killed.	F/S Slezak Killed.
F/S Potter Killed.	F/S Swansburgh Killed.
Sgt. Knox Killed.	Sgt. Titus Killed.
Sgt. Wood Killed.	Sgt. Watson Killed.
Sgt. Myers Prisoner of War.	Sgt. MacAuley Killed.
Sgt. Prentice Killed.	Sgt. Creede Killed.
Sgt. Withers Killed.	P/O Street Killed.
	P/O Laing Killed.

27th July, 1942

Funeral of F/S Thurlow, Sgt. Apperson. Sgt. Owens, F/S Albright and P/O Strong held at Barmby Moor.

29th July, 1942

2 aircraft in sea search. Nothing found.

Views of Pocklington in 1985. Scene of the crash of K on 24th July

29th-30th July, 1942

Saarbrucken (Burbach Steel Works). 8 aircraft. One did not start. All bombed the target some coming as low as 4 000 ft. Considerable damage done. One aircraft which arrived over the target late stated fires could be seen 75 miles away. Opposition slight.

31st July, 1942

Dusseldorf. 14 aircraft. 2 did not start. One returned early after being forced to jettison due to engine failure. A very successful attack. No cloud and only slight haze. Some pilots reported "A small Cologne." Intensive flak.

Two aircraft failed to return.

(T)	(S)
F/O West Prisoner of War.	Sgt. Hunter Killed.
F/O Bandeen Prisoner of War.	Sgt. O'Brien Killed.
Sgt. Gibbon Prisoner of War.	Sgt. Anderson Killed.
P/O Nadeau Died of wounds while a Prisoner of War.	Sgt. Bond Killed.
P/O Howard Prisoner of War.	Sgt. Irish Killed.
P/O Watters Killed.	Sgt. Laughlin Killed.
P/O Pearce Evaded capture.	Sgt. Woodman Killed.
Returned to U.K.	

3rd August, 1942

2 aircraft were detailed for a daylight raid on Hamburg which it was assumed would be under cloud cover. However, both aircraft turned back at the enemy coast as weather was still clear. Both aircraft flew up and down enemy coast for 90 minutes before returning to base. (The next daylight raid on Germany from Pocklington did not take place until the 24th June, 1944).

Daylight raid near Elvington. The enemy aircraft was pursued by fighters. No casualties but a number of bombs fell on Beverley Market Place.

4th-5th August, 1942

Essen. 5 aircraft. One returned early. This aircraft had port outer engine fail but carried on for 37 minutes until rising temperatures on the remaining 3 engines forced it to return. Target covered by cloud and bombed by "Navigational Aids." No results observed. 2 aircraft damaged by flak which was intense at the target.

5th August, 1942

One aircraft engaged in sea search. Nothing found after a 4 hour search. W/C Fauquier awarded the D.F.C.

6th-7th August, 1942

Duisburg. 6 aircraft. One returned early due to failed coolant gauges. Target obscured by haze but numerous scattered fires seen. The aircraft which returned early swung off the runway, collided with 2 Wellingtons causing considerable damage but only one injury.

One aircraft was attacked by an ME110 which damaged the rudder, petrol leads and tyres. Fire was not returned but a parachute was distinctly seen.

7th August, 1942

No 405 Squadron moved from Pocklington to Topcliffe.

No 102 Squadron arrived from Driffield under the Command of W/C S.B. Bintley A.F.C.

No 405 Squadron operated with 4 Group until October 1942 when it was detached to Coastal Command until February 1943, then it was transferred to No. 8 (Pathfinder) Group. The Squadron had the distinction of being the only Canadian Squadron in Pathfinder Command. Squadron personnel were awarded 9 D.S.O.'s, 161 D.F.C.'s, 24 Bars to D.F.C., 38 D.F.M.'s, 2 C.G.M.'s, 2 B.E.M.'s and 11 Mentions in Despatches.

9th-10th August, 1942

Osnabruck. (The first No 102 Squadron operation from Pocklington). 6 aircraft. One did not start and one returned early with unserviceable turret and landed at Linton. All bombed the target but haze and inaccurate marking made the aiming point difficult to identify. No definite results.

One aircraft did not return.

RB 211 (A)

P/O McLeod Prisoner of War.
P/O Lamont Prisoner of War.
Sgt. Long Prisoner of War.
Sgt. Richards Prisoner of War.
P/O McCarthy Killed.
Sgt. Willshire Killed.
Sgt. Jones Prisoner of War.

11th-12th August, 1942

Mainz. 5 aircraft. One returned early with turret trouble. The rest bombed successfully. There were several fires seen.
Le Havre. One "Freshman" aircraft. Successful attack. On return aircraft from both operations diverted to Linton on Ouse or Eastmoor.

12th August, 1942

Squadron stood down for one weeks intensive training. (It is believed that this was to train navigators in the use of "Gee").

Whitley from 24 O.T.U. Honeybourne crashed into hillside near Kirkby-Under-Dale. The Air Bomber Sgt. James was killed. The port engine of this aircraft caught fire and it crashed attempting an emergency landing at a "Q" Site.

15th August, 1942

Anti-invasion exercise held.

16th August, 1942

Funeral of Sgt. James held at Barmby Moor.

18th August, 1942

One aircraft swung badly on landing collapsing undercarriage and one landed heavily at Marston Moor also collapsing undercarriage.

20th-21st August, 1942

2 aircraft despatched on a leaflet raid to unoccupied France. One returned early owing to an unserviceable intercom but still dropped leaflets.

22nd August, 1942

One aircraft on cross country exercise crashed at Bluith Wells. Engine failed and feathering action was unsuccessful. No serious injuries.

28th August, 1942

No 10 Squadron commenced operations from Pocklington until runways completed at Melbourne.

28th-29th August, 1942

Saarbrucken. 4 aircraft of No 102 and 5 of No 10 Squadron. 2 did not start, one due to taxiing accident at Melbourne and the other with a constant speed unit unserviceable. One aircraft brought it's bombs back as compasses unserviceable. Haze made identification of target difficult but 2 aircraft claimed a successful attack. Fires were seen but bombing was generally scattered. One aircraft shot down a single engined night fighter off the German Coast.

One aircraft attacked by a night fighter wounding the rear gunner Sgt. Storey. This aircraft crash landed at Honington to get Sgt. Storey to hospital, but he died later.

1st-2nd September, 1942

Saarbrucken. 8 aircraft of No 102 and 4 of No 10 Squadron. 2 did not start. 3 returned early one of which crash landed at Low Catton injuring the bomb aimer. One took off late and was unable to maintain flight plan and the third had engine trouble. One aircraft brought bombs back as time limit of attack had expired.

The rest believed they had bombed the target in good visibility against only slight opposition. Later photographs however, showed the non-industrial town of Saarlouis and surrounding villages had actually been attacked. (The inhabitants of Saarlouis were able to take cover in the West Wall or Siegfried line which ran round the village).

2nd-3rd September, 1942

Karlsruhe. 4 aircraft of No 102 and 3 of No 10 Squadron. One did not start. The rest identified the target and saw bombs bursting in the town centre. Flak light and inaccurate.

4th-5th September, 1942

Bremen. 6 aircraft of No 102 and 3 of No 10 Squadron. One did not start. Weather clear with slight haze and bombing well concentrated. One aircraft shot down a JU 88 on the way back.

This raid was the first to use what was to become the standard P.F.F. technique of "Illuminators" (Flares) followed by "Visual Markers" (Coloured Flares) and "Backers Up" (Incendiaries).

4th September, 1942

Conversion flight aircraft collapsed undercarriage on heavy landing.

5th September, 1942

Defence exercise held. The Station was attacked by the 70th (Kings) Regiment but was successfully defended by Station Personnel.

Wellington aircraft from Snaith force landed at Hays Farm, Melbourne killing the rear gunner P/O Parry. The remainder of the crew suffered only slight injuries.

6th-7th September, 1942

Duisburg. 10 aircraft of No 102 and one of No 10 Squadron. 2 did not start. Flares scattered over the whole area and ground obscured by haze. Results appeared inconclusive but it was later found that this had been the heaviest raid on this target so far.

One aircraft landed at Manston with flak damage.

One aircraft of No 10 Squadron did not return.

W 7767 (Q)

P/O Morgan Killed.
Sgt. Billing Killed.
Sgt. Morris Killed.
Sgt. Rice Killed.
F/S Milne Killed.
Sgt. Henry Killed.
Sgt. Loveday Killed.

8th September, 1942

No 76 Squadron Halifax from Middleton St George crashed between Gate Helmsley and Stamford Bridge due to photo flash exploding in the bomb bay. All crew killed. Sgt. Nicholson, F/S Thompson, P/O Robson, Sgt. Harvey, Sgt. Stevens, Sgt. Murray and Sgt. Rumble.

Black-out week organised by W.A.A.F. who volunteered to repair black-out curtains throughout the camp.

8th-9th September, 1942

Frankfurt. 11 aircraft of No 102 and 3 of No 10 Squadron. 2 did not start. 2 returned early both with engine trouble. One bombed Darnstadt and 1 Mainz.

The remainder claimed to have bombed the target but later P.R.U. reports showed that Russelheim (Home of Opel Cars) was attacked. One aircraft sighted JU 88 on homeward trip. Rear gunner fired 3 x 2 second bursts and enemy aircraft broke away (Claimed as damaged). Moderate flak.

One aircraft swerved on landing and hit stationary aircraft. No casualties.

One aircraft of No 102 Squadron did not return.

W 7677 (Q)

Sgt. Farrell Killed.
Sgt. Phillips Killed.
Sgt. Barclay Killed.
Sgt. Griffiths Evaded capture. Arrived back in U.K. 6.12.42.
Sgt. Heap Evaded capture. Arrived back in U.K. 1.11.42.
Sgt. Whitfield Prisoner of War.
Sgt. Wright Prisoner of War.

10th-11th September, 1942

Dusseldorf. 10 aircraft of No 102 and 7 of No 10 Squadron. 2 did not start and one returned early with coolant trouble. One bombed Heerdt and the rest the primary. Ground haze but P.F.F. placed flares accurately and fires at the target aided navigation. Considerable heavy flak. This was the first raid on which Pathfinders used "Pink Pansies."

One aircraft of No 102 Squadron did not return.

W 7752 (R)

F/O Smith Killed.
Sgt. Marshall Killed.
F/S Pargher Killed.
Sgt. Moore Killed.
Sgt. Jackson Killed.
P/O England Killed.
Sgt. Schofield Killed.
P/O McCormack Killed.

13th-14th September, 1942

Bremen. 10 aircraft from No 102 and 7 of No 10 Squadron. 4 did not start. One returned early due to a glycol leak. Owing to strong north east winds all aircraft flown light to Eastmoor as it was considered inadvisable to take off from Pocklington towards the hills.

This was a successful attack doing considerable damage. Large fires were seen. Opposition intense.

All aircraft diverted on return. One crash landed near Coltishall injuring three of the crew. The bomb aimer Sgt. Rowe who had been wounded died later in hospital. One aircraft also crash landed at West Raynham but the crew were unhurt.

14th-15th September, 1942

Wilhelmshaven. 3 aircraft of No 102 and 6 of No 10 Squadron. One did not start. Target claimed attacked although covered with 7- 9/10 cloud. Flares appeared to be of little value but some fires and one large explosion seen. The P.F.F. marking was however accurate and this was the heaviest raid on this target to date. Flak was reported as unexceptional.

15th September, 1942

First 102 Squadron Dance held in the Officers Mess.

16th-17th September, 1942

Essen. 4 aircraft of No 102 and 4 of No 10 Squadron. One did not start and 3 returned early one with an oil leak and 2 with engine trouble. Target obscured by haze so aircraft bombed on E.T.A. and "Navigational Aids". Although only small scattered fires seen this was a most effective attack on this difficult target. Accurate heavy and light flak. Numerous searchlights.

On return all aircraft were diverted to Eastmoor as an "Early Return" had overshot due to U/S brakes blocking the main Hull/York Road.

18th September, 1942

Conversion flight aircraft taxied into tail of another. Pilot mistook rear light of other aircraft for taxi light.

18th-19th September, 1942

One aircraft despatched to drop leaflets in the Vichy/Clerdon region of France. Very little opposition.

19th-20th September, 1942

Saarbrucken. 9 aircraft of No 102 and 5 of No 10 Squadron. 3 returned early one damaged by photo flash exploding and the other 2 had an oxygen failure and coolant leak respectively. Remainder attacked the target which was obscured by haze. One large and several small fires seen but attack generally scattered. Opposition negligible.

On return one aircraft hit a tree in the Grassington area. As a result this aircraft was only able to climb in right hand circles. All the crew baled out successfully from 700 ft. except the navigator Sgt. McDougal who was killed. The aircraft crashed in West End village.

23rd September, 1942

Revue entitled "Take Off" given by R.A.F. and W.A.A.F. personnel to a large appreciative audience.

23rd-24th September, 1942

Flensburg (Submarine Yards). 8 aircraft of No 102 and 1 of No 10 Squadron. One returned early due to radio being put unserviceable by electrical storm. Visibility excellent and only moderate flak. Bomb bursts reported right across the target and large fires seen.

One aircraft attacked by ME 110. Fire was returned and pieces seen to fly off the tail. Claimed as "damaged".

2 aircraft of No 102 Squadron failed to return.

W 1239 (G)   W 1055 (F)

F/O Mee Killed.   P/O Bassom Killed.
Sgt. Wood Killed.   Sgt. Cooper Killed.
Sgt. Jonstone Killed.   F/S Reynolds Killed.
F/S Davidson Killed.   Sgt. Sherrard Smith Killed.
Sgt. Youmans Killed.   Sgt. Stainton Killed.
Sgt. Jackson Killed.   F/S Bennet Killed.
Sgt. Coulthard Killed.   Sgt. Gould Killed.
Sgt. Spirit Killed.

26th-27th September, 1942

Flensburg. 7 aircraft of 102 and 3 of 10 Squadron. Weather deteriorated and all aircraft recalled and diverted to Leconfield. One aircraft shot down a night fighter off the Danish coast after having been fired on by a flak ship.

27th September, 1942

F/L McClean missing since attack on Essen on the 8th June lectured aircrew on his escape from Holland. Repeated lecture on the 29th September at Melbourne.

1st-2nd October, 1942

Flensburg. 4 aircraft of 102 and 5 of 10 Squadron. One did not start. Crews were briefed to fly below 3 000 ft. to within 70 miles of the Danish coast and then descend to cross Denmark as low as possible. Climbed to avoid flak ships in the Little Belt and then bomb in a shallow dive to about 1 000 ft. then fly out to sea as low as possible.

Though this attack was effective nearly half the force involved, 12 aircraft out of 27 failed to return.

Six aircraft failed to return.

W 7858 (R)
102
F/Sgt. Matthews Killed.
Sgt. Dunn Killed.
Sgt. Peters Killed.
Sgt. Sadler Killed.
Sgt. Parker Killed.
Sgt. Tarver Killed.
Sgt. Bennet Killed.

(J)
10
Sgt. Campbell Killed.
Sgt. Smythson Killed.
Sgt. Goulay Killed.
Sgt. Stewart Killed.
Sgt. Sullivan Killed.
Sgt. Ivers Killed.
Sgt. Moore Killed.

W 1066 (H)
10
F/S Moller Killed.
Sgt. Hunter Killed.
Sgt. Pickard Killed.
Sgt. Brett Killed.
Sgt. McPherson Killed.
W/O Hughes Prisoner of War.
Sgt. McArthur Prisoner of War.

W 1066 (H)
102
F/S Cato Killed.
Sgt. McIntire Killed.
Sgt. Robinson Killed.
Sgt. Millbank Killed.
F/O McGillivray Killed.
Sgt. James Killed.
Sgt. Tooth Killed.

(M)   W 7717 (G)

10   10

F/O Jones Killed.	F/S Hayes Prisoner of War.
Sgt. Pickering Killed.	Sgt. Caplann Prisoner of War.
Sgt. Mawbury Killed.	Sgt. Pettican Killed.
Sgt. Stevens Killed.	W/O Matthews Prisoner of War.
Sgt. Prior Killed.	Sgt. Narregaard Killed.
Sgt. Curran Killed.	F/S Robinson Prisoner of War.
Sgt. Carter Killed.	W/O Steel Prisoner of War.

2nd-3rd October, 1942

Krefeld. 7 aircraft of No 102 and one of No 10 Squadron. One did not start. 2 returned early one with engine trouble and the other due to inaccurate compass. The remainder claimed to have attacked the primary target but although some good sized fires were seen this attack was scattered.

One aircraft of No 10 Squadron did not return.

W 116 (P)

P/O Baxter Prisoner of War.
F/O Armstrong Prisoner of War.
Sgt. Bradburn Prisoner of War.
Sgt. Clerke Prisoner of War.
Sgt. Lang Prisoner of War.
W/O Shan Prisoner of War.
Sgt. Stocks Prisoner of War.

5th-6th October, 1942

Aachen. 10 aircraft of No 102 and 4 of No 10 Squadron. One did not start. 4 returned early 2, with engine trouble, one with faulty intercom and one with unserviceable artificial horizon. Another aircraft was forced to jettison and return with navigational difficulties. The weather was not favourable with severe storms icing and an electrical storm approaching the target which was covered by 8-10/10 cloud.

Some crews managed to bomb through gaps in the cloud but little ground detail could be seen and the attack was scattered. Opposition light.

2 aircraft of No 102 Squadron did not return.

(C)	(O)
P/O Williams Killed.	W/O Shaw Killed.
Sgt. Thorpe Killed.	F/S McCowan Prisoner of War.
P/O McRae Killed.	F/O Marsh Prisoner of War.

Sgt. Morgan Killed.
Sgt. O'Connell Killed.
Sgt. Scott Killed.
Sgt. Bourne Killed.

Sgt. Meagher Prisoner of War.
Sgt. Levente Escaped
 & returned to U.K.
Sgt. Metcalfe Prisoner of War.
Sgt. Cailes Escaped & returned to UK
Sgt. Register Prisoner of War.

6th-7th October, 1942

Osnabruck. 6 aircraft of No 102 and 3 of No 10 Squadron. 2 did not start and one returned early due to magneto trouble. Haze prevented observation of ground detail but attack was accurate and well concentrated. Light flak, some fighters seen but no combats.

10th-11th October, 1942

Terschelling (Minelaying). 5 aircraft of 102 and 5 of 10 Squadron. This was the first minelaying operation carried out by either Squadron. Quiet and uneventful trip. Slight flak. A few fighters seen but no combats.

13th-14th October, 1942

Kiel. 10 aircraft of 102 and 11 of 10 Squadron. 4 returned early. One due to damage by flak, one with the rear turret unserviceable and one with overheating oil temperature and one with engine trouble. This appeared to be a successful attack but many bombs were drawn away by a decoy site.

Intense accurate heavy flak. Some fighters seen and 2 aircraft had inconclusive combats.

One aircraft which had returned early due to partial failure of the starboard inner engine was unable to climb high enough to jettison bombs so was forced to land well overweight. This caused the aircraft to bounce badly and swing off the runway and catch fire. The crew were unhurt but the airfield was unserviceable for several hours.

The Flight Engineer of one aircraft Sgt. Wilkinson was severely wounded by flak.

One aircraft of No 10 Squadron did not return.

W 7870 (G)

P/O Lindsey Killed.
Sgt. Hogan Killed.
Sgt. Dunegeld Killed.
F/O Bradley Killed.

Sgt. Girdlestone Killed.
Sgt. Gregg Killed.
Sgt. Lancton Killed.

The only known WWII colour photograph of the Halifax in flight.
Reproduced in B/W   *R.A.F. Museum*

15th-16th October, 1942

Cologne. 10 aircraft of No 102 and 8 of No 10 Squadron. 2 returned early one due to getting badly off track and the other due to intercom trouble. This was a disappointing attack. Cloud over the target varied from nil to 10/10 with strong winds not according to forecast, scattering P.F.F. Flares which together with dummy fires attracting many bombs.

One aircraft of No 10 Squadron did not return.

W 1058 (S)

W/C Wildy (C.O. of No 10 Squadron) Killed.
F/L Davies (Senior Navigation Officer) Prisoner of War.
F/L Brindley (Gunnery Leader) Killed.
Sgt. Dubroy Killed.
F/O Murphy Prisoner of War.
F/S Harrison Prisoner of War.
P/O Sanderson-Miller Prisoner of War.
Sgt. Burkinshaw Killed.

18th October, 1942

Conversion flight aircraft swung violently on take off, collapsing undercarriage. Pilot was distracted by top hatch blowing off.

19th October, 1942

Mr. P. Morgenthau United States Secretary of State visited Pocklington accompanied by the A.O.C. A.V.M. Carr.

21st October, 1942

The aircrew of No 10 Squadron gave a party for the ground crews in the N.A.A.F.I. at Melbourne.

22nd October, 1942

Social evening held in the N.A.A.F.I. at Melbourne to select performers for the Station Concert Party.

23rd-24th October, 1942

Genoa. (No 10 Squadron commenced operations from Melbourne on this day). 11 aircraft. One returned early with exactor trouble. Weather clear en route but a bank of cloud over the target extended for some distance inland. P.F.F. Flares inaccurate and Savona received most of the bombs meant for Genoa. Flak inaccurate and no searchlights.

On return 2 aircraft which were diverted to Holme on Spalding Moor collided on the runway. The crew of one aircraft DT212(Q) were unhurt but the pilot of the other, W 1181, W/C Bintley, the C.O. of No 102 Squadron was killed and the Wireless Operator F/O Graham died later in York Military Hospital. This accident appeared to be due to a burst tyre on W/C Bintley's aircraft causing it to swing and collide with the other aircraft.

24th-25th October, 1942

Milan. 3 aircraft. One returned early due to icing. The remaining 2 believed they had attacked the target but low cloud made identification impossible so crews were forced to bomb on E.T.A. and the glow of fires from a daylight raid by Lancasters on the 24th. Little damage done.

Scattered inaccurate flak at the target. Fighters seen but no combats.

26th October, 1942

W/C G.W. Holden D.F.C. took command of No 102 Squadron.

27th October, 1942

Funeral of W/C Bintley and F/O Graham held at Barmby Moor.

30th October, 1942

One aircraft badly damaged when it left the runway following a violent swing on take off.

2nd November, 1942

Conversion flight aircraft damaged. Swung off runway and undercarriage collapsed. Pilot was distracted by close proximity of the Watch Tower.

3rd November, 1942

Further aircraft damaged. Duplicate of accident on the 2nd November.

6th-7th November, 1942

Ameland (Minelaying). 5 aircraft. 2 brought their mines back as they could not obtain an accurate pinpoint in spite of going down to 400 ft. Quiet uneventful trip.

7th November, 1942

Beaufighter from Church Fenton crashed near Bielby. Sparks from faulty exhaust manifold caused pilot to shut down engine and was then unable to maintain height on one.

Pilot Sgt. Griffith killed. Observer Sgt. Wheatland in hospital with burns and fractured pelvis.

7th-8th November, 1942

Genoa. 15 aircraft. 2 did not start. One returned early as air speed indicator unserviceable. This was a most successful attack. Aircraft being airborne for over 10 hours. Later photo reconnaissance showed smoke rising from centre of city. Defences saturated early on in the attack and fires visible from the Alps on the way back.

Weather bad on return and aircraft diverted all over the country.

9th-10th November, 1942

Hamburg. 10 aircraft. 2 returned early one with rear turret unserviceable and the other was forced to jettison when taking violent evasive action from 5 JU 88's. Heavy cloud and a change of wind caused the target to be totally obscured and bombing was done on "Navigational Aids" and was as a result widely scattered.

S.O.S. received by Hull with only part of call sign discernable. Unsuccessful sea search carried out next day.

2 aircraft failed to return.

(A)	(F)
Sgt. Marler Killed.	Sgt. Neville Killed.
P/O Zealand Killed.	Sgt. Featherstone Killed.
Sgt. Callan Killed.	P/O Dunlop Killed.
Sgt. Broome Killed.	Sgt. Sidercheck Killed.
Sgt. Moir Killed.	Sgt. Riddle Killed.
Sgt. Richardson Killed.	Sgt. Brook Killed.
Sgt. Kingsland Killed.	Sgt. Hope Killed.
Sgt. Read Killed.	Sgt. Player Killed.

13th November, 1942

No 10 Squadron aircraft landed at Pocklington "Wheels Up".

15th-16th November, 1942

Genoa. 12 aircraft. 11 reached and bombed the target in good conditions. All aircraft obtained target photographs within 1.1/2 miles of the aiming point and some within a few hundred yards. One aircraft had a "hang up" and jettisoned in the channel on the way home and one returned from the target on 3 engines and landed at Tangmere.

16th-17th-18th November, 1942

Exercises held with Home Defences. In all cases aircraft had little difficulty in evading searchlights but were picked up by night fighters using "Special Equipment".

18th-19th November, 1942

Turin. 5 aircraft. 2 were forced to jettison with engine trouble. Only slight haze. P.F.F. Flares clearly seen and no difficulty experienced in identifying target. Many fires seen. Flight unexceptional.

20th-21st November, 1942

Turin. 9 aircraft. 2 returned early one due to W.T. being unserviceable and the other due to a manipulative failure by the Flight Engineer. 10/10 cloud from York to the Alps but cleared once mountains were crossed. Bomb bursts and fires seen over a wide area of the city. Successful attack. Four No 50 Squadron Lancasters landed at Pocklington owing to bad visibility at their own base. The S.A.S.O. Group Captain E.J. Brooks flew as P2 in W/C Holden's aircraft on this operation.

22nd November, 1942

One aircraft had engine fire but was landed without further damage or casualties "Superb Airmanship".

22nd-23rd November, 1942

Stuttgart. 10 aircraft. One did not start. One returned early due to the port outer engine failing after take off. Bombs were jettisoned to maintain height. Thick cloud from the Humber to the French Coast and 5/10 cloud over the target with thick ground haze. P.F.F. Flares not well concentrated but most bombs appeared to fall in the general area of the city. Fires visible up to 70 miles away. Opposition moderate some heavy flak. Some fighters seen but no combats.

One aircraft failed to return.

(A)

P/O King Killed.
F/O Follet Killed.
Sgt. Clarkson Killed.
Sgt. Thompson Killed.
Sgt. Johnson Killed.

Sgt. Cheetham Killed.
Sgt. Nicholson Killed.

23rd-24th November, 1942

Terschelling (Minelaying). 5 aircraft. 2 aircraft of No 158 Squadron at Rufforth also operated from Pocklington but returned to Rufforth. Successful operation except for one which brought mines back having been caught by searchlights and defences were therefore warned.

25th November, 1942

Officers Mess at Elvington held a house-warming party attended by officers from Pocklington and Melbourne.

25th-26th November, 1942

Ameland (Minelaying). 2 aircraft. Both Successful. Quiet uneventful trip.

26th-27th November, 1942

Frisian Islands (Minelaying). 6 aircraft, together with 4 from No 158 Squadron. One brought mines back as unable to obtain an accurate pinpoint, low tide making identification of ground detail difficult.

Opposition intense at South Ameland and Nordeney. One aircraft landed heavily on return damaging undercarriage.

28th November, 1942

F/L Davies accidentally shot himself in the foot while trap shooting. (Shotgun found to have a faulty safety catch). Taken to York Hospital and foot amputated.

28th-29th November, 1942

Turin. 10 aircraft. Only 6 took off when the perimeter track was blocked by an aircraft which had a puncture.

4/10 cloud at the target. Attack well concentrated. Flak inaccurate and a few inconclusive combats with night fighters.

2nd-3rd December, 1942

Frankfurt. 12 aircraft. Bad haze over the target reflected flares and the aiming point could not be identified resulting in a badly scattered attack.

One aircraft, unable to identify the target sought an alternative north west of Kaiserlautern. Dropped high explosives from 1 500 ft. and incendiaries from 900 ft. while rear gunner shot up stationary train. No results observed.

Only one aircraft landed at Pocklington on return. The rest scattered all over the country.

Three aircraft failed to return.

W 7916 (L)

W/C Embling (C.O. of 77 Squadron) Prisoner of War.
S/L Walkington Killed.
P/O Haines Evaded capture and returned to U.K.
F/S Fantini Prisoner of War (F/S Fantini had the misfortune to land in a Luftwaffe Camp).
Sgt. Johnson Prisoner of War.
Sgt. Molloy Killed.
Sgt. Law Killed.
Sgt. Douglas Prisoner of War.

W7913 (L)	W7883 (H)
Sgt. Morrissy Killed.	Sgt. Charman Prisoner of War.
Sgt. Kenyon Killed.	P/O McKim Prisoner of War.
P/O Pike Killed.	Sgt. Nutter Prisoner of War.
Sgt. Brown Killed.	(Wounded).
Sgt. Robson Killed.	Sgt. Pope Killed.
Sgt. Taylor Killed.	Sgt. Edwards Killed.
Sgt. McCallum Killed.	Sgt. Neilson Prisoner of War
Sgt. Allbrecht Killed.	Sgt. May Prisoner of War.

6th-7th December, 1942

Mannheim 12 aircraft. Weather prevented any accurate pin pointing and Pathfinder flares scattered over a wide area. Fair amount of heavy flak. One aircraft attacked by 3 night fighters on the run in but shot 2 down.

2 aircraft failed to return.

W7924 (E)	W7911 (B)
Sgt. Buchwalter Killed.	Sgt. Grant Killed.

74

Sgt. Jones Killed.
Sgt. Pendelpho Killed.
Sgt. Hawke Killed.
Sgt. Pinkney Killed.
Sgt. Sannholm Killed.
F/S Carr Killed.

Sgt. Brownhill Killed.
Sgt. MacCartney Killed.
Sgt. Eden Killed.
Sgt. Jackson Killed.
Sgt. Langford Killed.
Sgt. Clements Killed.

8th-9th December, 1942

Juist Baltrun. (Minelaying). 8 aircraft. One did not start. Mines laid accurately. Flak more active than usual.

One aircraft failed to return.

W7925 (S)
Sgt. Ketchell Killed.
Sgt. Haig Killed.
Sgt. Parry Killed.
Sgt. Hopwood Killed.
Sgt. Box Killed.
Sgt. Adams Killed.
Sgt. Massey Killed.

9th-10th December, 1942

Turin. 8 aircraft plus one of No 76 Squadron from Linton-on-Ouse. One returned early due to excessive fuel consumption. This attack was a failure due to the weather. Heavy cloud and haze over the target. Flak had increased but searchlights useless.

10th December, 1942

A.C. Bird and A.C. Parker admitted to York Military Hospital following a road accident outside the guardroom.

11th-12th December, 1942

Turin. 8 aircraft. One returned early with engine trouble. This attack was a failure due to weather. Heavy cloud and haze over the target.

Visibility closed down on return and aircraft diverted all over the country.

One circled base and was diverted to Middleton St. George and descended through cloud to check position only to crash into the hills at Dowthwaite Farm, Hawnby near Helmsley. All on board Sgts. Morgan, Wooley, Casson, Allen, McPhee, Lines and Norris were killed.

Aircraft J flown by F/L Milnes was hit by flak at 17 000 ft. after crossing the Alps. This put the starboard outer engine unserviceable and the aircraft spun down to 13 000 ft. The bombs were jettisoned and the aircraft turned back. At 5 000 ft. near Amiens was again hit by flak which stopped both port engines. Height was lost to 2 000 ft. when the port inner engine re- started. Carried on 2 engines (Port and starboard inner) and was picked up and followed by 2 fighters from Paris but they did not attack. On crossing the Channel further burst of flak blew off the port outer engine.

This aircraft crash landed at Bradwell Bay with no hydraulics injuring the Flight Engineer, Sgt. McMillan, demolishing an army hut and causing some casualties to army personnel.

The Station Operations Record Book rightly describes this flight as an epic.

One aircraft landed "wheels up" at Scampton. Pilot was distracted by the large number of aircraft in the circuit.

14th-15th December, 1942

Terschelling (Minelaying). 6 aircraft. One did not start. The rest laid mines accurately. Little opposition. Night fighters seen but no combats.

20th December, 1942

Cpl Stagg admitted to Station Sick Quarters with Sub Arachnoid Haemorrhage. In spite of artificial respiration being carried out for 15 hours he died the next day.

20th-21st December, 1942

Duisburg. 7 aircraft. Very successful attack, visibility excellent and the target easily identified by Pathfinder flares. Defences heavy at first but weakened towards the end of the attack. One aircraft was attacked by a night fighter and believed to have shot it down. 2 target photographs showed aircraft silhouetted below.

24th December, 1942

Cpl Riley W.A.A.F. fell off her bicycle in Pocklington village. Admitted to York Military Hospital with fractured skull.

25th December, 1942

Christmas Day. Officers and Sergeants served Christmas Dinner to Airmen. Dances held in all Messes.

17/18 April 1942 TOTAL WAR !!
The Canadian's last operation with Wellington (Wimpy) aircraft was a raid on Hamburg. A warehouse containing 60,000 bottles of alcohol was bombed.

(Rear Gunner to Pilot - The Germans must be short of ammunition, they are shooting bottles at us !)

Cartoon by F/O John J. Jamieson DFM.

This is the one with the hiccuping engines

The Wellington was nicknamed after a character in Popeye cartoons. This was a prodigious eater of hamburgers named J. Wellington Wimpy.

1943

An early production Halifax

By 1943 ultimate victory was in sight. On the Eastern Front the Germans were being pushed back, Stalingrad had been recaptured with over 284 000 men either killed or Prisoners of War. By May the Germans in Africa had surrendered and Allied troops were back on European soil with the invasion of Sicily. Italy had surrendered and had declared war on Germany. In the Far East the Japanese had been stopped and the Americans were advancing slowly across the Pacific but at sea the U Boats were still on the offensive. In two convoys in March 40 U Boats had sunk 22 out of 90 ships.

Bomber Command was now well on the offensive. The famous Dambuster raid took place in June. The "Firestorm" raid on Hamburg in July caused over 20 000 deaths. Peenemunde was badly damaged in August and in November the Battle of Berlin began.

The Americans had also joined in the attack on Germany with a daylight raid on Huls in June. In August however they suffered heavy losses in a joint attack on Schweinfurt and Regensburg. Schweinfurt was attacked again in October but again losses were heavy; 77 aircraft out of a force of 291 did not return.

LIE IN THE DARK AND LISTEN
By Noel Coward
Lie in the dark and listen
It's clear tonight so they're flying high
Hundreds of them, thousands perhaps
Riding the icy, moonlit sky
Men, machinery, bombs and maps
Altimeters and guns and charts
Coffee, sandwiches, fleece lined boots
Bones and muscles and minds and hearts
English saplings with English roots
Deep in the earth they've left below
Lie in the dark and let them go
Lie in the dark and listen.

Lie in the dark and listen
They're going over in waves and waves
High above villages, hills and streams,
Country churches and little graves
And little citizens' worried dreams
Very soon they'll have reached the sea
And far below them will lie the bays
And cliffs and sands where they used to be
Taken for summer holidays
Lie in the dark and let them go
Theirs is a world we'll never know
Lie in the dark and listen.

Lie in the dark and listen
City magnates and steel contractors
Factory workers and politicians
Soft hysterical little actors
Ballet dancers, reserved musicians
Safe in your warm civilian beds
Count your profits and count your sheep
Life is passing over your heads
Just turn over and try to sleep
Lie in the dark and let them go
There's one debt you'll forever owe
Lie in the dark and listen.

6th January, 1943

One aircraft force landed at Huby near Eastmoor. Violent vibration but the pilot was unable to identify so feathered both port engines but was then unable to maintain height. No injuries.

9th-10th January, 1943

Frisian Islands. (Minelaying). 11 aircraft. One returned early due to an oil leak in the port inner engine. Mines laid accurately. Crews reported "black out" in Denmark practically non existent.

10th January, 1943

Cpl. Dobbs struck by propellor of aircraft as he was attempting to cross runway. Killed instantly.

14th-15th January

Lorient. 11 aircraft. 2 did not start. 3 returned early due to engine trouble. No results observed in very bad weather and only a few target photographs obtained in the whole command.

Aircraft diverted all over the country on return.

15th-16th January, 1943

Lorient. 5 aircraft. One returned early due to loose hatch. Visibility fair. P.F.F. flares released dead on time and all crews claimed to have identified the target and this was a more accurate attack then the previous one. Opposition light. Night fighters sighted but no combats.

One aircraft from No 51 Squadron (Snaith) crashed at Pocklington with damaged flaps. No casualties.

16th-17th January, 1943

Berlin. 5 aircraft. Aircraft were to have their dorsal turrets removed but in the event only one ready.

This operation was regarded as having a high nuisance value and attracted an enormous amount of flak and searchlight opposition but due to the long distance involved and the weather at the target, the damage was only slight.

The only aircraft from Pocklington was hit by flak which damaged the rudder controls and petrol leads but landed successfully at Oakington by "Skilful Airmanship".

17th-18th January, 1943

Berlin. 4 aircraft. One returned early due to glycol leak. Thick cloud all the way. The target was clear of cloud but obscured by haze. Pathfinder flares late and as a result attack scattered.

Flak not heavy at start of attack but became heavy and accurate towards the end. One aircraft attacked twice by a night fighter which broke away after gunners had fired 2 bursts.

23rd-24th January, 1943

Lorient. 7 aircraft. Good visibility. Well concentrated attack. Opposition moderate but some heavy flak.

27th-28th January, 1943

Dusseldorf. 11 aircraft. One did not start. One returned early with intercom trouble. Large fires seen in spite of 10/10 cloud. Opposition moderate but some heavy barrage flak. 5 fighters seen but only one inconclusive combat.

This was the first raid in which "Ground Marking" was carried out by Mosquito Aircraft equipped with Oboe and resulted in considerable damage.

One aircraft failed to return.

W 7918

F/L Lindsay Killed.
F/O Colquhoun Prisoner of War.
Sgt. Turner Prisoner of War.
Sgt. Thompson Prisoner of War.
Sgt. Bennett Killed.
F/L O'Hanley Killed.
W/O Thomas Prisoner of War.

30th-31st January, 1943

Terschelling. (Minelaying). 3 aircraft. Mines laid accurately. Considerable amount of light flak but no aircraft hit.

2nd February, 1943

Searchlight co-operation exercise held. "Black out" in Goole, York, and Leeds reported to be ineffective.

2nd-3rd February, 1943

Cologne. 14 aircraft. One did not start. 8 bombed the primary but due to poor weather and scattered flares this was a disappointing attack. Defences moderate.

One aircraft failed to return.

W 7882 (P)

F/S Ross Thompson Killed.
Sgt. Goffin Killed.
Sgt. Watt Killed.
Sgt. Naylor Killed.
Sgt. Lillywhite D.F.M. Killed.
Sgt. Gwillian Killed.
Sgt. Guerrier Killed.

3rd-4th February, 1943

Hamburg. 6 aircraft. 2 did not start. 2 were forced to jettison in bad weather due to turrets icing up. The remainder bombed on sky markers. Though this attack was regarded as abortive, some damage was done.

One aircraft failed to return.

W 7821 (M)

Sgt. Lofthouse Killed.
Sgt. Haxby Prisoner of War.
Sgt. Alexander Killed.
Sgt. Thompson Killed.
Sgt. Short Killed.
Sgt. Crouch Prisoner of War (Wounded).
Sgt. Winnard Prisoner of War.

4th-5th February, 1943

Turin. 6 aircraft. One returned early due to a glycol leak. Visibility very good over the target. All attacked primary causing considerable damage.

Pathfinder flares effective.

Defences had increased since previous attack but still inaccurate. Dummy fires seen but easily identified.

Lorient. One aircraft. This was an all incendiary attack starting large fires. This aircraft operated with No 77 Squadron on their first operation from Elvington.

6th-7th February, 1943

St. Nazaire and Texel. (Minelaying). One aircraft. Mines laid as ordered. Opposition moderate, flak ships operating off the coast.

7th-8th February, 1943

Lorient. 10 aircraft. Cloud cleared 30 miles from the target. Mass of fires seen on both sides of the river. A devastating attack with negligible opposition.

9th-10th February, 1943

Searchlight co-operation exercise held. It was felt that this was of benefit to both aircrew and ground defences. Black out reported poor at Hull and Sheffield.

11th-12th February, 1943

Wilhemlshaven. 6 aircraft. One returned early with engine on fire too low to jettison or bale out. This aircraft crashed at North Dalton. The second pilot Sgt. Hill survived with concussion but the rest of the crew, Sgts. Saunders, Washbourne, Reilly, Cooper, Coles, Amos and F/O Farquaharson-Ley were killed.

2 aircraft were forced to jettison owing to severe icing and the remainder bombed on sky markers which the Pathfinders had dropped on H2S fixes. Though only flashes could be seen through cloud this was later found to have been an accurate effective attack.

Opposition moderate. Searchlights unable to penetrate cloud.

13th-14th February, 1943

Lorient. 11 aircraft. All bombed in excellent conditions doing much damage. This was the first occasion on which 1000 tons of bombs were dropped on one target.

466 aircraft were involved in this operation. 164 Lancasters, 140 Wellingtons, 96 Halifaxes, and 66 Stirlings. 3 Wellingtons, 2 Lancasters, One Halifax and 1 Stirling were lost.

14th-15th February, 1943

Cologne. 10 aircraft. One did not start. One was destroyed when the incendiaries fell off during bomb check. The crew managed to evacuate the aircraft in time. One returned early after jettisoning bombs over Germany as the aircraft was unable to climb. The remainder bombed on sky markers as no ground detail visible and this operation met with limited success. Flak moderate. Many sightings of night fighters.

One aircraft attacked by a JU 88 and 2 ME 110's. The rear gunner scored hits on one ME 110 which was seen to dive away in flames. This was in spite of only 2 guns working and the remaining 2 jamming during the attack. One aircraft also attacked by a Stirling.

One aircraft failed to return.

W 7880 (J)
F/L Hartshorn Killed.
Sgt. Cheasman Killed.
F/S Conner Killed.
Sgt. Gilbert Killed.
F/S Farah Killed.
Sgt. Kilyon Killed.
Sgt. Cox Killed.

16th-17th February, 1943

Lorient. 9 aircraft. A most successful attack. The target which contained the main U Boat pens was now completely devastated and deserted.

Many night fighters seen and one claimed shot down.

18th-19th February, 1943

Wilhelmshaven. 9 aircraft. One returned early due to the doors blowing off the rear turret. Marker flares clearly seen in good visibility but no enthusiastic reports of good results and no large fires seen.

This attack fell to the west of the target.

Many night fighters seen but no combats. Considerable light but only moderate heavy flak.

Backtrum. (Minelaying). 2 aircraft. Successful operation.

19th-20th February, 1943

Wilhelmshaven. 10 aircraft. One returned early due to engine cowling lifting off and one bombed Island of Spiekeroog owing to unserviceable constant speed unit.

This attack was reported as concentrated but fell to the north of the target.

One night fighter attacked and several sighted. One unidentified aircraft seen to blow up over the target. Opposition about the same as previous attack but more accurate flak.

25th-26th February, 1943

Nuremburg. 11 aircraft. 2 returned early due to severe icing and one crashed at Baldiss Hall Farm near Colchester probably as a result of losing control in bad weather. All crew killed. Sgts. Bray, Herbert, Smith, Dudley, Sanitsky, Widgery and Barfoot.

One aircraft had A.S.I. "Ice-Up" over the Thames Estuary, but continued to the target and back to the French coast before the A.S.I. started working. In spite of this the Navigator coped well.

The Pathfinder flares were late and the main force had to wait. Most of the bombs fell to the north of the target and on the neighbouring town of Furth but some damage was done.

Flak heavy at first but lessened. Some fighters seen but no combats.

26th-27th February, 1943

Cologne. 8 aircraft. One did not start. Crews again had to wait for Pathfinder flares but later attack well concentrated. Some large fires seen.

Opposition moderate until target indicators fell then it lessened.

2 aircraft failed to return.

HR 669 (E)

Sgt. Gibbons Killed.
Sgt. Langham Killed.
P/O Dowdall Killed.

W 7919 (N)

Sgt. Frith Killed.
P/O Burgher Killed.
Sgt. Cox Killed.

Sgt. Richins Killed.
Sgt. Hunt Killed.
Sgt. Russell Killed.
Sgt. Wilson Killed.
Sgt. Bradshaw Killed.

Sgt. James Killed.
Sgt. Wilby Killed.
Sgt. Peake Killed.
Sgt. Stewart Killed.

One aircraft detailed for minelaying operation crashed on take off. Crew unhurt.

27th-28th February, 1943

Searchlight co-operation exercise held. Leeds blackout reported poor.

28th February - 1st March, 1943

St. Nazaire. 10 aircraft. All attacked the target, the next most important U Boat base after Lorient. A most successful attack, large fires seen and defences swamped. Moderate accurate heavy flak. Some fighters seen but no combats.

One aircraft hit by incendiaries from another aircraft. This was stated to be "Normal Operational Hazard".

1st-2nd March, 1943

Berlin. 6 aircraft. All bombed and returned safely. P.F.F. flares successfully marked both the route and the target itself and were visible for 150 miles. Large explosion seen as last aircraft left. Flak light to moderate. Surprising absence of night fighters.

An H2S set taken from a Stirling shot down near Rotterdam on which the Germans were working was destroyed in this raid. However, an almost intact set was recovered from a Halifax which crashed in Holland enabling the Germans to continue their research.

2nd March, 1943

Halifax of 1652 H.C.U. (Marston Moor) swung following heavy landing. Undercarriage collapsed.

3rd-4th March, 1943

Hamburg. 8 aircraft. 2 returned early one with intercom trouble and the other with a sick crew member. One was forced to jettison owing to oxygen failure, the Captain collapsing just before the aircraft reached the target.

CAPTAIN .... NAVIGATOR Sgt FENTON .... 2nd PILOT ....

CREW B/A SGT AUSBROOK

SPECIAL S/C ....

ORDERS ....

			MOON				TWILIGHT	

SUN			MOON				TWILIGHT	
RISES	SETS	RISES	SETS				A.M.	P.M.

Gaining
Fast / Slow sec./hour Losing

RATE

WATCH AT .... G.M.T. XB 263 ?

T.O.T. 21.19 - 21.35
CONCENTRATIONS EGMOND-14 15,000 20.48
03 02 E 12,000 OCT 10,000 22.26

H/A 19 20
S/C 19-40
82?

LR MILES

FORECAST WINDS

STAGE	FROM 2,000 FT.		6,000 FT.		10,000 FT.		51,000 FT.	
	FROM	TO	FROM T.	SPEED	FROM T.	SPEED	FROM T.	SPEED
	300	15	+1	280	25	-4	280	10	7	240	79
							20,000 240 65

WEATHER FORECAST

A too 2330 ARMED
B 045
C too
D 080 ← James II

FROM TO	W/V USED	HEIGHT FT.	T.A.S.	RQD. TRACK (T)	COURSE (T)	VAR.	COURSE (M)	D.R. G/S	DIST.	TIME
BASE	290		120							
HORNSEA	20	4,000	166	092	089	11	100	186	26	8
AKUNEER	280	8,000	118	115	118	10	128	212	144	40
02 80 E	35		103	115	119	8	124	225	45	19
02 00 E	275	13,000	105.8							
51 40 04 34	240	16,000	209	133	131	7	138	252	119	28
EGMOND	240		212	145	189	7	196	212	15	43
51 40 06 58	55	14,000	160-1							
KATSEN	240		240	020	010	7	014	236	22	5
TARGET	43	14,000								
51 44 04 11	246		240	290	292	7	299	198	123	38
WHITLEY	35	14,000								
EGMOND	280		198	295	293	9	302	174	214	45
SEARNSEA	22	5,000								
HORNSEA	300		190	242	244	11	285	198	26	83
HORNSEA	8	2,000								
BASE										

TIME	RQD. TRACK (T)	W/V USED AND D.R. DRIFT	Course (T)	Course (M)	NAVIGATIONAL OBSERVATIONS (Pin-points, Fixes, Position Lines, Actual T.M.G., Actual Drift, G/S and W/V, Manoeuvres, etc.)	GENERAL OBSERVATIONS (Met. Conditions, Bombing, Intelligence, Enemy Action, etc.)	I.A.S. corr. for Inst. & Position Error	HEIGHT & TEMP.	TAS	D.A. G/S	DIST. TO RUN	D.A. TIME	E.T.A.
19					WATCHES SYNCHRONISED	AR CONT'ON' G. CHECKED							
20					BKB & GNE	IFF 'ON'							
19	115 092	090-20	092	103	BASE S.L HORNSEA			158 4500 166 184			26	19	19.05
50	115	085-25	119	129	DR HORNSEA S/B 03 90 E			158 1200 148 200			119	23	19.55
50					BEACON 53' HEAD 201 × 119								
					320 BON NU ALT 140°(T)								
20 02					FIX 53 43N 00 46 E	B 2 N C 136/60							
20 064					FIX 53 38N 01 04 E	B 2.5N C 42.19							
20 11					FIX 53 33N 01 26 E Aircraft turn	B 2.9N C 42.46							
					A 15 T W5 G/S then -OK								
20 4					BEACON 59 HEAD 193 × 119								
					312 BON NU Alt 132 (T) Turns Q								
20 20					BEACON 55 HEAD 110 × 119								
					229 BON NU ALT 049°(T)								
20 24					FIX 53 04N 01 51 E LOOP fix — 1Min								
					FIX 52 09N 02 42 E	B 4 46 C 40 98							
20	115	260	121	129	A 600 T 15 G/S 246 DR 03 00E S/C EGMOND	ICE OF		156 -17m 201		440	14 23 20 29.35		
					WN DR 133 Aircraft						79 19 20		
20 40					FIX 52 49N 03 55 E	A 5.22 C 39.66							
20 45					1ST ORBIT COMMENCED SHIVER B								
					A 32								
20 48					1ST ORBIT CEASED				209 32 8 20 W8			
20	511 123	149-55 124	134		AR EGMOND S/C DORTTEN COAST BELOW		163 18 cm 212 165 119 24 22 18						
					WN 124 134 Aircraft	Flak to ST							20 51
21 02						AMMMM ?							
						G LIGHTS FLASH							
16						RED FLARES TO P							
						YELLOW FLARES TO ST							

Time		Notes / Event	Nav data					
21.24		BOMBS GONE	Ht 16,000 Hdg 190 TAS 212					
21.25		BOMB DOORS CLOSED						
21.26	1022	TARGET S/E HALTERN	186 R...0 240 252 22 5 21					
		Violent evasive action – compass not maintained						
21.34 298	35 294 301	A/C HALTERN S/E EGMOND	186 R...0 246 210 123 35 22					
21.39								
21.44		HICKELS GONE						
21.56			B210 46 13 22					
21.08 295	25 293 202	FIX 54 30N 05 04E EGMOND s/c HORNSEA B.5-49 C.38-18 Nose Down 2000 ft	186 Sea 198 174 24 75 22					
		W/V 290 30 Airplot						
23.19		FIX 52.49N 04 00E						
22.20		SANER 'OFF B.5.24 C.29.62						
23.26		FIX 55 02N 03 24E B.4.99 C.40.24						
22.323		FIX 53 11N 03 04E B.4.40 C.40.43						
22.26.20		HO POLARIS 53 15 mis.						
24.21.30		HO POLARIS 52 57 mis.						
22.40		FIX 52 21N 02 32E B.3.90 C.41.43						
22.U130		HO POLARIS 53 12. WN 255 326 Airplot						
23.50 269	35 282 292	DR 22 33N 02 02E a/c HORNSEA	186 Sea 198 166 95 34 23 2					
22.56		FIX53 3HN 01 29 E B 2.90 C.42.71						
23.04		FIX53 38N 00 53 E A 2.59 C.43 56	160 50 143 23 2					
23.17		A/C T.R. G/S 160						
23.18		FIX 53 50.. 00 02 5 B. 2/5 A 51-19						
23.22 242	15 244 288	CATFOSS BEACON AHEAD HORNSEA C/E BASE	186 2000 190 176 26 82 22 2					
23.24		BAKE BEACON TO PORT						
23.30		Batt						
23.37		landed						

Markers dispersed at first but concentrated later, however, later photographs showed Wedel 10 miles west of the target had been attacked but nevertheless some bombs did fall on Hamburg.

Fighters seen but no combats.

Frisian Islands. (Minelaying). 3 aircraft. Mines laid on fixes from "Navigational Aids".

5th-6th March, 1943

Essen. 12 aircraft. All attacked the target. Weather clear to Dutch coast then only 3/10 cloud at the target. Target indicators well concentrated and large explosion seen. Fires visible from the Dutch coast. Searchlights numerous but ineffective. Intense heavy flak. Many night fighters seen but no combats.

Friesian Islands. (Minelaying). One aircraft. Successful operation. Slight opposition from flak ship.

7th-8th March, 1943

Frisian Islands. (Minelaying). One "Freshman" aircraft. This aircraft was engaged by a flak ship as it was approaching the dropping point. Forced to jettison mines live and return on 3 engines.

8th-9th March, 1943

Nuremburg. 11 aircraft. Route markers accurate but target markers badly scattered. Attack widely dispersed.

Opposition moderate, fighters seen but no combats though a number of aircraft were seen falling in flames.

One aircraft failed to return.

JB 840 (N)

Sgt. Hibben Prisoner of War.
Sgt. Slocombe Prisoner of War.
Sgt. Simpson Prisoner of War.
Sgt. Atkinson Prisoner of War.
Sgt. Sawkins Prisoner of War.
Sgt. Hughes Prisoner of War. (Escaped and returned to U.K.).
Sgt. Mansford Prisoner of War. (Escaped and returned to U.K.).

9th-10th March, 1943

Munich. 9 aircraft. One returned early with engine trouble and 2 were forced to jettison. Pathfinder flares on time but main force late. Attack well concentrated in good weather. Defences not unduly troublesome.

Many fighters seen and one claimed shot down.

11th-12th March, 1943

Stuttgart. 11 aircraft. One returned early with glycol leak. Bombed on ground markers. Target appeared to be well covered with incendiaries but this was not a successful attack partly due to the Germans using dummy target indicators for the first time. Moderate heavy and considerable light flak. Fighters seen but no combats.

12th-13th March, 1943

Essen. 12 aircraft. One did not start. No cloud, good visibility. Heavy flak in Durston Hallen area. The target on this occasion was very accurately marked and considerable damage done. Most of the bombs falling right across the giant Krupps Factory.

One aircraft badly shot up by night fighter badly wounding the rear gunner. This aircraft landed at Docking to get the rear gunner to hospital.

One aircraft also hit by incendiaries from another aircraft.

3 aircraft did not return.

JB 836 (T)

F/O Barnes Killed.
Sgt. Thurlow Killed.

P/O Beeton Killed.

Sgt. Elkins Killed.
Sgt. Quinliven Killed.
Sgt. Lowdell Killed.
Sgt. Felsenstein Killed.

DT 739 (P)

Sgt. Charlesbois Killed.
Sgt. Horne Prisoner of War. (Injured).
Sgt. Hedges Prisoner of War. (Slight Injury).
Sgt. Powers Prisoner of War.
Sgt. Hughes Killed.
Sgt. Kemp Prisoner of War.
Sgt. Williams Prisoner of War.

DT 799 (L)

Sgt. Newland Killed.
Sgt. Floyd Killed.
Sgt. Druette Killed.
Sgt. Crow Killed.
Sgt. Beaven Killed.
Sgt. Jones Prisoner of War.
Sgt. Haigh Killed.

22nd March, 1943

G/C North Carter D.F.C. posted in as Station Commander.

24th March, 1943

6 Wellington aircraft of No 466 Squadron landed at Pocklington after minelaying operation.

26th-27th March, 1943

Duisburg. 13 aircraft. 10/10 cloud over the target compelled the main force to bomb on sky markers. The resulting attack was badly scattered but this was partly due to 5 of the Oboe Mosquito's being forced to return and one being shot down out of a force of 9.
Moderate to intense heavy flak. Several aircraft damaged. 2 aircraft hit, one of which landed at Coltishall to get injured Navigator Sgt. Moore to Hospital. The other returned to base on 3 engines.

27th-28th March, 1943

Berlin. 8 aircraft. Pathfinders had marked 2 areas but both were well short of the city, however, many fires were observed over a wide area. By chance the main weight of the attack fell on a secret Luftwaffe stores depot at Tetlow 11 miles south west of the centre of Berlin. This destroyed a large quantity of radio, radar and other technical stores.

2 aircraft had minor flak damage.

28th-29th March, 1943

St. Nazaire. 7 aircraft. Good visibility except for ground haze and possible smoke screens. Pathfinder flares well concentrated in dock area resulting in a well directed attack. Little opposition.

29th-30th March, 1943

Berlin. 10 aircraft. 3 returned early due to icing and one (JB 848) crashed at West Green soon after take off killing all the crew. F/S Comrie, P/O Harper, Sgts. Dorrington, King, Squires, McGraith and P/O Jenkins. This aircraft had to take violent evasive action for a Melbourne aircraft and control was lost.

The weather forecast for this attack was inaccurate resulting in scattered attack. Defences active but no fighters seen. Several aircraft damaged by flak.

3rd April, 1943

Pocklington, Melbourne and Elvington Airfields formed into Bomber Command "Clutch" under the Command of Air Commodore G.A. (Gus) Walker (In 1985 "Gus" Walker returned to Pocklington and Melbourne airfields to attend a dedication service and unveil memorials to the crews from both Stations. After a long and distinguished career he retired from the R.A.F. in 1970 with the rank of Air Chief Marshal. He died on the 11th December, 1986). At the time of his appointment to Pocklington he was the youngest Air Commodore in the R.A.F.

Gus Walker (second from left) talking to aircrew.
Can anybody identify the other people in this photograph ?   IWM Copyright

3rd-4th April, 1943

Essen. (Krupps Works). 13 aircraft. Bombing scattered at first but later concentrated doing considerable damage. Some crews reached target with little opposition but others were singled out for attack. Several fighters seen, 2 inconclusive combats. Several aircraft damaged by flak and P/O McLoughlin the rear gunner of L killed by flak over the target.

4th-5th April, 1943

Kiel. 11 aircraft. Heavy cloud and strong winds compelled aircraft to bomb on sky markers. No results seen except for glow reflected in cloud. Attack widely scattered. Moderate opposition.

8th-9th April, 1943

Duisburg. 7 aircraft. 2 returned early as they were unable to maintain height due to icing. Cloud tops to 20 000 ft. with varying degrees of icing forced crews to bomb on E.T.A. No results seen and bombing widely scattered. Flak intense and accurate.

10th April, 1943

Sir Archibald Sinclair (Air Minister) visited Station and lunched in the Officers Mess. A.O.C. 4 Group A.V.M. Carr also present.

10th-11th April, 1943

Frankfurt. 12 aircraft. One returned early with glycol leak. Rest bombed on dead reckoning in 10/10 cloud with tops to 10 000 ft. resulting in a badly scattered attack.

One aircraft had 1000 lb bomb "hang up" so brought it back. One aircraft reported being fired on by a 4 engined aircraft to port and below. A single burst put port inner constant speed unit unserviceable. A third aircraft also complained there was a considerable amount of flak over Kent on return.

14th-15th April, 1943

Stuttgart. 12 aircraft. One returned early due to compass trouble and one returned having been damaged by flak on the way to the target and landed at Oakington.

No cloud, good visibility. All aircraft could see the markers which were accurate at first but later became scattered resulting in bombs falling to the north west of the target. However, later photo

12.3.43	12 aircraft detailed to attack ESSEN. Weather: No cloud and good visibility in target area.			at TRAFFORD.	314
	SGT. V.C.ACK. SGT. L.C.BROWN.				
V.7927	F/L L.F.H.INGRAM. SGT. L.C.RICHARDS. SGT. L.D.GARLICK. SGT. H.A.PUDD. SGT. J.MOULSONG. SGT. K.J.WILLIAMS. P/O. K.K.HUSHBROOK. SGT. K.K.BROWN.	1920	2338 As above	Attacked primary target at 17,000 feet heading 180°T HS 115. No cloud good visibility. Saw white T.I. markers at DUTEN on approach and red T.I. at target followed by green. Red T.I. markers in bomb sights. Many sticks of bombs seen to fall in well concentrated area. Many fires starting, glow seen when crossing coast on homeward journey.	
JB. 779	P/O. L.G.MOFFATT. P/O. J.P.KEZINGER. SGT. P.G.RICKEY. P/O. C.DAVIES. SGT. W.J.McLAM. SGT. G.C.COWAN. SGT. D.F.MOON. SGT. B.W.THOMAS.		As above	Scrubbed owing to coolant leak.	
W.7883	P/O. M.S.HARTLEY. SGT. W.H.HUGHES. SGT. J.F.THOMSON. SGT. A.HICKS. SGT. J.MEES. SGT. J.R.TAANNERY. SGT. H.J.HOOPER.	1922	0006 As above	Attacked primary target at 16,000 feet heading 189°M HS 170. No cloud good visibility. Red T.I. markers at target men falling. Red and green T.I. markers in bomb sights. On arrival whole target area covered in fires. At 2135 enormous explosion occurred in target area with red flame shooting up to 4/5000 feet. Smoke and glow seen when crossing Dutch coast on homeward journey.	
HR.667	F/S. W.R.CURRIE. P/O. D.W.HARPER. SGT. W.C.C.POTTERTSON. SGT. W.C.C.SOUTERS. SGT. J.KING. SGT. J.W.McCRATH. P/O. W.H.JENKINS.	1927	0014 As above	Attacked primary target at 18,000 feet heading 180°M HS 214. Nil cloud good visibility. Identified red T.I. markers. T.I. markers in bomb sights, own results not seen. Other explosions and fires seen. Small flak holes in fuselage sustained over target. Bombing well concentrated.	
HR.741	SGT. R.B.HALE. SGT. R.F.MUIR. SGT. W.A.HODGES. SGT. W.HALLOWS. SGT. A.J.M.DOOLEY. SGT. F.M.SMITH. P/O. E.D.WILCOCK.	1921	2355 As above	Attacked primary target at 17,000 feet, between red and green T.I. markers. Attacked by E/A on run in at 2117 rear gunner wounded in leg and face. Fuselage holed in many places. Intercom, hydraulics A.S.I. u/s. Control tubes, elevators and rudder damaged, trimmer A cable to elevator and IFF aerial cut. Tail tyre burst, landed at DOCKING to get rear gunner to hospital.	
V.7934	F/S. J.H.McCORMACK. SGT. W.T.LAMBERT. SGT. A.CURTIS. SGT. T.M.HOUSDER. SGT. M.HALE. SGT. D.A.FIELD.	1924	2341 As above	Attacked primary target at 15,000 feet heading 160°M HS 210. Clear small amount of ground haze. Identified white markers on approach and red and green over target. Green T.I. markers in bomb sights. Large fires concentrated in small area, two large explosions seen.	

recoconnaissance showed considerable damage had been done.

16th-17th April, 1943

Pilsen. (Skoda Works). 14 aircraft. This attack was carried out at a fairly low level. One aircraft came down to 4 000 ft. and shot up a goods train on leaving target. The markers for this raid were dropped in error and Dorbrey received most of the bombs meant for Pilsen.

One aircraft failed to return. It was flown by S/L Lashbrook who was just starting his second tour after Commanding the Conversion Flight.

This aircraft was attacked by a night fighter over the Belgian/French Frontier near Chimney Forest. The rear gunner P/O Williams was killed and the mid upper Sgt. Neil wounded. The port wing and both engines were set on fire. The Captain ordered the crew to "Bale out" at about 7 000 ft. Sgt. Neill managed to escape through the rear entrance hatch and the remainder through the front hatch. The Flight Engineer F/S Knight handed the Captain his parachute before baling out himself at about 3 000 ft., the Captain leaving at 500 ft. or less.

Sgt. Neill spent the rest of the War as a Prisoner but the rest of the crew initially evaded capture.

S/L Lashbrook hid out for 4 days and then contacted the Resistance F/S Knight was picked up by the Germans in Paris in July and became a Prisoner for the rest of the War. S/L Lashbrook, Sgt. Laws (W/Op), F/L Bolton (Navigator) and F/O Martin (Air Bomber) evaded capture and returned to the U.K. in May and June 1943. S/L Lashbrook and F/O Martin met on a Paris Station in early June and came home together.

Mannheim. 1 "Freshman" aircraft. This attack a diversion for the Pilsen raid was very effective. This aircraft damaged by flak produced an aiming point photograph only 2 miles from the aiming point. "Good show" by an inexperienced crew.

20th April, 1943

W/C H.R. Coventry took command of No 102 Squadron.

20th-21st April, 1943

Stettin. 15 aircraft. One returned early with rear turret unserviceable and oxygen trouble. Water features at target clearly seen and markers accurate. Though the target was more than 600 miles from England and well out of Oboe range this was a most successful attack. One aircraft reporting fires visible from 100 miles on the way home.

2 aircraft failed to return.

DT 747 (P)
Sgt. Griffiths Killed.
Sgt. Bennett Killed.
Sgt. Marsh Killed.
Sgt. Jenkinson Killed.
Sgt. Weir Killed.
Sgt. White Killed.
Sgt. Smith Killed.
Sgt. Campbell Killed.

HR 712 (M)
Sgt. Oliver Prisoner of War.
Sgt. Doidge Killed.
F/S Bartman Killed.
Sgt. Day Killed.
Sgt. Irving Killed.
Sgt. Meldrum Prisoner of War.
Sgt. Warner Killed.

26th-27th April, 1943

Duisburg. 15 aircraft. One returned early with oxygen trouble. One had bombs "hang up" over the target. No ground detail seen and success depended on the accuracy of the target indicators.

They were in fact to the north east and this raid was regarded as only a partial success.

Defences active, several aircraft hit by flak and one attacked by a night fighter. 4 aircraft returned on 3 engines.

One aircraft failed to return.

JB 918 (T)

Sgt. Grainger Killed.
Sgt. Oatridge Killed.
Sgt. Willis Killed.
Sgt. Beck Killed.
Sgt. Wells Killed.

Sgt. Harris Killed.
Sgt. Foley Killed.

27th-28th April, 1943

Frisian Islands. (Minelaying). 6 aircraft. All laid mines successfully by dead reckoning from a Gee fix.

28th-29th April, 1943

Kattegat. (Minelaying). 9 aircraft. All laid mines successfully by dead reckoning from a pin point on the coast. (207 aircraft were engaged on this operation and the 593 mines laid were the greatest so far. However, 22 aircraft did not return, the heaviest loss in minelaying operations of the whole war).

Searchlight co-operation exercise held. One aircraft flew Base - Newcastle - Northampton - Nottingham - Base, but only picked up by 3 searchlights for 2 minutes and these lost after mild evasive action.

30th April-1st May, 1943

Essen. (Krupps Works). 12 aircraft. One did not start (taxied into unlit W.T. Van) and 3 returned early one due to hatch blowing off and the other 2 with low oil pressure. 10/10 cloud with tops to 14 000 ft. Aircraft bombed on release point markers and one aircraft reported it could see 12 aircraft silhouetted in the target area. Most bombs fell on the city but with no general concentration.

2nd May, 1943

2 aircraft collided on the perimeter track with only minor damage.

4th-5th May, 1943

Dortmund. 17 aircraft. One did not start. 2 returned early with engine trouble.

A successful attack, the first major one on this target. Fires could be seen from the Zuyder Zee on the way home. Moderate heavy flak.

One aircraft (F/S Bowman) was forced to ditch 75 miles from the coast. The crew were all rescued the following morning. The records are confused at this point but it would appear that an aircraft of Coastal Command dropped an airborne lifeboat which the crew boarded and from which they were picked up by Air Sea Rescue Launch. The crew only suffered slight injuries.

2 aircraft failed to return.

JB 869 (H)   HR 667 (U)

Sgt. Happold Killed.   S/L Flowerdew Killed.
Sgt. Barratt Prisoner of War.   P/O Grant Killed.
Sgt. Brownlie Prisoner of War.   Sgt. Dutton Killed.
Sgt. Jones Prisoner of War.   F/S Buck Killed.
Sgt. McGregor Killed.   Sgt. Rose Killed.
Sgt. Bowles Killed.   F/O Baxter Killed.
Sgt. Tiller Killed.   P/O Chiverton Killed.

5th May, 1943

Viscount Trenchard "The Father of the Royal Air Force" visited Pocklington.

One aircraft swung on take off collapsing undercarriage.

7th May, 1943

Station visited by A.O.C. Bomber Command Air Marshal Harris accompanied by A.O.C. 4 Group A.V.M. Carr. Stayed for lunch and addressed crews.

One aircraft crash landed in a field following engine failure. No injuries.

12th-13th May, 1943

Duisburg. 12 aircraft. One returned early with artificial horizon unserviceable. The markers were well placed resulting in a very successful attack. Large explosions and fires could be seen from Amsterdam on the way home. Intense heavy flak.
One aircraft failed to return.

JB 799 (E)

F/S Moffat Killed.
F/O Erzinger Killed.
Sgt. Hurle Killed.
P/O Davies Killed.
Sgt. Holman Killed.
Sgt. Cowan Killed.
Sgt. Moon Killed.

13th-14th May, 1943

Bochum. 13 aircraft. 3 returned early. One due to unserviceable compass and the other 2 with engine failure and a sick navigator respectively. Pathfinder flares easily seen but decoy markers drew much of the bombing away from the main target. Flak moderate to intense.

One aircraft ditched off Yarmouth after being shot up over the target but the crew were rescued by an M.T.B. with only slight injuries.

One aircraft failed to return.

JB 964 (G)

Sgt. Hatchard Killed.   Sgt. Lee Killed.
F/O James Prisoner of War.   Sgt. Brown Killed.
Sgt. Leedham Killed.
Sgt. Coughlin Prisoner of War.
Sgt. Fowles Killed.

15th-16th May, 1943

Searchlight co-operation exercise held. One aircraft flew Base, Out to Sea, Mablethorpe, Manchester, South Wold, Out to Sea, Flamborough, Hull, Lissett, Base. Aircraft held by searchlights for 5 minutes. Enough to dazzle pilots and gunners.

16th-17th May, 1943

Practice parachute attack alarm held and another searchlight co-operation exercise held. 2 aircraft flew Base, Isle of Wight, Edinburgh, Trowbridge, Birmingham, Middlesborough, Base. Only "flick-over" from searchlights but both were intercepted by night fighters.

18th-19th May, 1943

Searchlight co-operation exercise held. 5 aircraft were detailed to fly Base, Spalding, Southwold, Out to Sea, Nottingham, Isle of Man, Belfast, Londonderry, Larne, Paisley, Edinburgh, Newcastle, Middlesborough, Hull, Base but were recalled from the Manchester area due to deteriorating weather. Only one aircraft coned, no fighters.

21st May, 1943

Major Southgate, Flak Liaison Officer gave a most interesting talk to aircrew.

23rd-24th May, 1943

Dortmund. 22 aircraft. "A notable effort". 2 returned early due to oxygen failure and generator not charging. Weather poor over target but markers accurate resulting in a successful attack. One aircraft had a near miss with bombs dropped from another aircraft and another was hit by a bundle of leaflets over the target. Flak not as intense as expected. Numerous night fighters sighted.

All aircraft diverted on return one of which had to land flapless due to flak damage to flaps and tailplane.

One pilot commented there were too many aircraft firing the colours of the day over the English coast on return.

One aircraft failed to return.
JD 112 (H)

F/S Sargent Prisoner of War.
Sgt. Campbell Killed.

Sgt. Galloway Prisoner of War.
Sgt. Newberry Killed.
Sgt. Smith Killed.
Sgt. Webb Prisoner of War.
F/O Bullock Killed.

25th-26th May, 1943

Dusseldorf. 21 aircraft. "A further notable effort". Not a well concentrated attack. Weather bad on return. All diverted.

27th-28th May, 1943

Essen. 20 aircraft. 2 returned early. Weather prevented this attack being concentrated and bombs fell over a wide area.

One aircraft failed to return.

JD 149 (H)

P/O Jeffrey Killed.
F/O Entwhistle Killed.
Sgt. Zareikin Killed.
Sgt. Lowings Killed.
Sgt. Heslop Killed.
Sgt. Smith Killed.
P/O Fewtrell Killed.

28th-29th May, 1943

Searchlight co-operation exercise held. One aircraft flew Base, Leicester, Stratford on Avon, Southend, Kew Bridge, Walton on the Naze, Northampton, Base. Only held by searchlights for a few seconds. Pilot was of the opinion that searchlights lacked cohesion.

29th-30th May, 1943

Wuppertal. 22 aircraft. 2 did not start. This attack was a great success. One aircraft reported a column of smoke to 12 000 ft. About 1 000 acres (80%) of the built up area was destroyed.

One aircraft attacked by 2 JU 88's one of which was showing a head light. The rear gunner fired 3 bursts and the flight engineer saw it catch fire. It was then seen burning on the ground by the Captain.

One aircraft failed to return.

W 7934 (J)

Sgt. Ware Killed.
F/O Allen Killed.
Sgt. Hartland Killed.
Sgt. Smith Killed.
Sgt. Stewart Killed.
Sgt. Hoddle Killed.
Sgt. Sheerman Killed.

8th June, 1943

Air Marshal Sir Philip Joubert (Inspector General) visited Pocklington, Melbourne and Elvington.

11th-12th June, 1943

Dusseldorf. 21 aircraft. Some aircraft were diverted by markers inadvertantly dropped early but the remainder carried out the most devastating attack on this target during the whole War. Smoke rose to 14 000 ft. and fires could be seen from the Dutch coast. Opposition moderate.

Bomb aimer of one aircraft and wireless operator of another wounded by flak.

12th-13th June, 1943

Bochum. 18 aircraft. One did not start. Target obscured by large patch of thin cloud but extensive damage caused due to accurate Oboe sky marking. Searchlights active. Moderate flak. Night fighters seen but no combats.

One aircraft failed to return.

JB 868 (T)

Sgt. Hale Killed.
Sgt. Woodley Killed.
Sgt. Muir Killed.
Sgt. Hobbis Killed.
Sgt. Hallows Killed.
Sgt. Quevillon Killed.
Sgt. Gibbs Killed.
F/O Wilcock Killed.

17th-18th June, 1943

Searchlight co-operation exercise held. 4 aircraft took part one of which was flown by Air Commodore Walker. ("Gus" Walker had lost his right arm in a desperate attempt to warn the crew of a burning Lancaster when he was Station Commander at Syerston. This did not stop him flying however).

18th June, 1943

Halifax from 1663 H.C.U. (Rufforth) swung on landing collapsing undercarriage.

19th-20th June, 1943

Le Creusot. 22 aircraft. Crews had difficulty in identifying the target and smoke caused trouble for later crews. Only about 1/5 of the main force managed to bomb the target, but most Pocklington aircraft achieved good results bombing from 4-9 000 ft. Searchlights and flak light. One aircraft returned on 3 engines and landed at Manston.

21st-22nd June, 1943

Krefeld. 19 aircraft. 2 returned early one with Gee U/S and the other due to intercom trouble and also having lost time after taking evasive action due to night fighter. Target accurately marked in good visibility. This was probably one of the most devastating attacks of the whole War. 705 aircraft took part 262 Lancasters, 209 Halifaxes, 117 Stirlings, 105 Wellingtons and 15 Mosquitoes.

The whole city centre was burnt out, 5 517 houses destroyed, 1056 people killed, 4 550 injured and 72 000 lost their houses.

Of the attacking force 17 Halifaxes, 9 Lancasters, 9 Wellingtons and 9 Stirlings were lost.

One Pocklington aircraft ditched close to the Dutch coast. The crew were spotted by Mustangs at 06.35 and Typhoons at 15.30. At 19.00 2 Walrus Amphibians of No 277 Squadron found them. 3 got into one aircraft and 4 into the other. 3 were landed at Martlesham Heath. The other aircraft was unable to take off so taxied until it met an M.G.B. which took them to Felixstowe.

22nd-23rd June, 1943

Mulheim. 16 aircraft. One returned early due to engine trouble. Clear weather. Accurate attack doing considerable damage. It was estimated that 64% of the town was destroyed. Intense flak. Fighters seen but no combats.

24th-25th June, 1943

Wuppertal. 18 aircraft. 2 returned early one with low oil pressure and one with a combination of low oil pressure and navigational trouble. A well concentrated attack doing much damage. Defences only moderate but night fighters active. One aircraft claimed to have damaged a night fighter which attacked it.

2 aircraft failed to return.

JB 834 (C)

Sgt. Marsden Killed.
F/O Lewis Killed.
Sgt. Barnes Killed.
Sgt. Hicks Killed.
Sgt. Warwick Killed.
Sgt. Ablett Killed.
P/O Perkins Killed.

JD 144 (U)

Sgt. Sheppard Killed.
Sgt. Tovey Killed.
Sgt. Gettings Killed.
Sgt. McDonald Killed.
Sgt. Clark Killed.
Sgt. Rushton Prisoner of War.
Sgt. Cole Prisoner of War.

25th-26th June, 1943

Gelsenkirchen. 16 aircraft. One returned early with starboard inner unserviceable. The Oboe equipment in 5 of the 12 Oboe Mosquitoes did not work resulting in poor target marking. Not a successful attack. Intense heavy flak. One aircraft shot down a night fighter which attacked it and another aircraft reported seeing lights in the form of a Cross of Lorraine over France. (The Cross of Lorraine was the emblem of the Free French Forces).

One aircraft failed to return.

JB 843 (F)

Sgt. Gore Killed.
Sgt. Wright Killed.
Sgt. Mitchell Killed.
Sgt. Gough Killed.
Sgt. Poskett Killed.
Sgt. Sugden Killed.
Sgt. Judd Killed.

28th-29th June, 1943

Cologne. 17 aircraft. One returned early with constant speed unit unserviceable. In spite of 10/10 cloud and several other setbacks this was a devastating attack striking the most powerful blow yet against the Ruhr and was Cologne's worst raid of the war. This attack consisted of 608 aircraft attacking in 8 waves of 4 minutes each. Heavy barrage flak up to 20 000 ft. Night fighters seen but no combats. One aircraft returned on 3 engines due to flak damage.

2nd July, 1943

One aircraft had a propellor come off during ground running of engine.

3rd-4th July, 1943

Cologne. 20 aircraft. One returned early with starboard inner unserviceable. Attack well concentrated in spite of intense heavy flak. Night fighter activity moderate.

One aircraft failed to return.

BB 428 (Q)

F/S Jenkins Killed.
P/O Hodgson Killed.
Sgt. Peck Killed.
Sgt. McConnell Killed.
Sgt. Watson Prisoner of War.
Sgt. Galloway Prisoner of War.
Sgt. Garlick Killed.

9th-10th July, 1943

Gelsenkirchen. 21 aircraft. Hazy cloud to 20,000 ft. caused this attack to be scattered with few aircraft seeing the target flares. Moderate to intense flak at target and night fighter activity in the Rennes area. 2 aircraft had inconclusive combats and one was fired on by another Halifax.

One aircraft failed to return.

BB 242 (Z)
F/S Fraser Killed.
Sgt. Stockton Prisoner of War.
F/S Mansell Killed.
Sgt. Glass Killed.
Sgt. Edwards Prisoner of War.
Sgt. Morse Killed.
Sgt. Brand Prisoner of War.

13th-14th July, 1943

Aachen. 23 aircraft. One returned early with compass and Gee unserviceable. Though crews reported target indicators as scattered in 10/10 cloud this attack did a considerable amount of damage. Slight flak. Searchlights non existant.

2 aircraft failed to return.

JD 297 (Q)
W/C Coventry (C.O. of No 102 Squadron Killed)
F/L King (Navigation Leader) Killed.
F/L Hogg (Gunnery Leader) Killed.
Sgt. Brown Killed.
Sgt. Hardy Killed.
Sgt. Pine-Coffin Killed.
F/O Read Killed.

JB 894 (X)
Sgt. Amos Killed
Sgt. Douthwaite Killed.
Sgt. Fradley Killed.
Sgt. Brown Prisoner of War.
Sgt. Raw Killed.
Sgt. J. Smith Killed.
Sgt. W. Smith Killed.

15th July, 1943

W/C F.A.C. Fowle took Command of No 102 Squadron.

15th-16th July, 1943

Montbeliard. 22 aircraft. Though this attack was carried out at a relatively low altitude the Peugot factory was only slightly damaged. Crashed aircraft burning on the ground was bombed by some aircraft.

Light flak towards the end of the attack. Few night fighters seen and one aircraft had inconclusive combat.

24th-25th July, 1943

Hamburg. 24 aircraft. A record for the Squadron. This was the first attack to use "Window" and a considerable amount of damage was done. Flak moderate. Searchlights numerous but not effective.
One aircraft failed to return.

DB 308 (X)

F/L Bakewell Killed.
F/S Cowin Killed.
P/O Smith Prisoner of War.

F/S Page Killed.
Sgt. Edwards Killed.
Sgt. Wood Killed.
Sgt. Swinton Killed.
P/O Hill Killed.

25th-26th July, 1943

Essen. 22 aircraft. 3 returned early due to glycol leak and engine failures. Weather hazy en route but fair at the target. Pathfinder flares accurate, large fires and explosions seen. Night fighters active, numerous combats seen and one aircraft successfully evaded a night fighter. Moderate flak at target. Searchlights ineffective.

One aircraft had oxygen supply fail just short of the target. The Captain and Navigator passed out. The Flight Engineer controlled the aircraft until they came round and another aircraft was struck by incendiaries.

Three aircraft did not return.

JD 150 (A)

Sgt. Brown Killed.
P/O Hitchcock Killed.
Sgt. Rooke Killed.
Sgt. Gough Killed.
Sgt. Sinclair Killed.
Sgt. Tyler Killed.
F/O Alison Killed.

JD 169(J)

Sgt. Whitehouse Killed.
P/O Smith Killed.
Sgt. Brown Killed.
Sgt. Evans Killed.
F/S Turner Killed.
Sgt. Spencer Killed.
F/L Moon Killed.

JB 864 (B)

F/O Clarke Killed.
Sgt. Thorne Prisoner of War.
Sgt. Bailey Killed.
Sgt. Harrison Killed.
P/O Slater Killed.
Sgt. Bartle Killed.
F/O Slipp Prisoner of War.

27th-28th July, 1943

Hamburg. 20 aircraft. One returned early due to engine trouble. good well co-ordinated attack with defences lighter than on the last occasion. Photographs showed large area of fires visible from 180 miles away and crews reported smoke to 20,000 ft. This was the first "Firestorm" raid.

(See Martin Middlebrook's book "The Battle of Hamburg"). 16,000 multi storey aprtment buildings were destroyed and about 40,000 killed and 200,000 (2/3rds of the polulation) fled the city.

2 aircraft did not return

JD 150(A)

Sgt. Brown Killed.
P/O Hitchcock Killed.
Sgt. Rooke Killed.
Sgt. Gough Killed.
Sgt. Sinclair Killed.
Sgt. Tyler Killed.
F/O Alison Killed.

JB 864(B)

F/O Clarke Killed.
Sgt. Bailey Killed.
Sgt. Thorne Prisoner of War.
Sgt. Harrison Killed.
P/O Slater Killed.
Sgt. Bartle Killed.
F/O Slipp Prisoner of War.

28th July, 1943

2 aircraft engaged in sea search for boat. One aircraft saw 2 high speed launches within 100 yards of boat which was displaying a message "Bring Boats". 12-13 people on board who were assumed to be refugees from occupied Europe.

29th-30th July, 1943

Hamburg. 21 aircraft. Large fires seen in south and south west side of the city. Flak moderate, searchlights numerous but ineffective. Numerous night fighters. One aircraft attacked by night fighter which damaged flaps and tail wheel.

2 aircraft failed to return.

HR 711 (C)

Sgt. Gaston Killed.
Sgt. Ball Killed.
Sgt. Williams Killed.
Sgt. Brown Killed.
Sgt. Veraas Killed.
Sgt. Yarwood Killed.
Sgt. Cocking Killed.

W 7883 (R)

F/S MacQuarie Killed.
Sgt. Whitley Killed.
Sgt. Wright Killed.
Sgt. Trehenann Killed.
Sgt. Morgan Killed.
Sgt. Woodroff Killed.
F/O Williams Killed.

31st July, 1943

The Medical Officer reported only one case of Pedicilous Pubis following F.F.I. for the whole Station.

2nd-3rd August, 1943

Hamburg. 20 aircraft. 2 returned early due to unserviceable radio controls and an oxygen leak. Weather very bad with cu-nimbs. from 10-20 000 ft. Attack not a success as many crews forced to jettison. Pathfinders tried both ground and sky marking but few crews reported seeing anything. One crew reported that bomb loads could be seen being jettisoned all the way from the coast to the target. Flak very light. Searchlights completely ineffective. Very few fighters seen.

6th August, 1943

One aircraft overshot due to faulty A.S.I.

9th-10th August, 1943

Mannheim. 16 aircraft. One returned early with compass trouble. One bombed Trier as a last resort after having been badly shot up by a night fighter. This attack was generally scattered but considerable damage was done over a wide area. Opposition light but night fighters active. 3 seen and one was claimed as "damaged".

The aircraft which returned early collided with a parked aircraft. No casualties.

2 aircraft failed to return.

JD 408 (R)

S/L Pestridge Prisoner of War.
P/O Hunter Prisoner of War.
F/S Walker Prisoner of War.
Sgt. Dunn Prisoner of War.
F/S Sherrington Killed.
F/O Burdon Killed.
F/O Bays Killed.
F/O West Killed.

JB 782 (W)

Sgt. Thomas Prisoner of War.
Sgt. Wilbraham Killed.
Sgt. Buffery Killed.
Sgt. Perry Prisoner of War.
Sgt. Wallis Killed.
Sgt. Lafford Killed.
Sgt. Marsh Killed.

10th-11th August, 1943

Nuremburg. 20 aircraft. 3 returned early one of which crashed just outside the airfield killing F/O Storey the Captain, Sgt. Bowers and Sgt. Newman and injuring the rest of the crew F/S Poulter, Sgts. McEwan, Lawman and Chappell.

The ground markers on this operation were obscured by haze but some damage was done. Flak slight. Night fighters not as numerous as usual.

One aircraft failed to return.

JD 369 (A)

Sgt. Ward Killed.
Sgt. MacLearnon Prisoner of War.
Sgt. Bostle Prisoner of War.
Sgt. Davey Killed.
F/S Shaw Killed.
Sgt. Irving Killed.
Sgt. Chapman Killed.
F/O Vivian Killed.

12th-13th August, 1943

Milan. 15 aircraft. One returned early due to a bad oil leak. This raid was considered to be a success. All aircraft had to be diverted to airfields in the south of England on return.

17th-18th August, 1943

Peenemunde. 17 aircraft. A "Splendid Success" in spite of fairly thick cloud over the target. This was the only occasion in the second half of the war when the whole of Bomber Command attempted a precision raid against a small target. It was also the first occasion on which a "Master Bomber" was used. (G/C J.H. Searby of No 83 Squadron).

This attack was carried out at a fairly low level with some aircraft coming down to 6 000 ft. and most below 10 000 ft. This halted the production of V.1's and V.2's for some months and probably permanently reduced production.

Aircrew on this raid were told they were attacking a Radar Research Unit the destruction of which would make life easier for them in the future, also that if this raid was not successful they would have to return until the target was destroyed.

On return one aircraft crashed at Ashbourne but the crew were unhurt.

This was also the first occasion in which the Germans used twin upward firing cannons in ME 110's. 2 of these "Schrage Musik" aircraft are believed to have shot down 6 returning bombers.

(For further details of this attack see "The Peenemunde Raid" by Martin Middlebrook published by Allen Lane).

22nd-23rd August, 1943

Leverkusen. 18 aircraft. Ground detail obscured by haze and most aircraft forced to bomb on E.T.A. Attack scattered but a few large fires seen. However, only a few bombs actually fell on the target. Moderate heavy flak. Searchlights ineffective. Many fighters seen but no combats.

One aircraft failed to return.

JD 378 (C)

S/L Jackson Prisoner of War.
F/O Booth Prisoner of War.
Sgt. Kaye Prisoner of War.
Sgt. Dolan Prisoner of War.
Sgt. Haynes Prisoner of War.
Sgt. Williams Killed.
Sgt. Vernon Prisoner of War.

23-24th August, 1943

Berlin. 21 aircraft. One returned early with Gee and Monica unserviceable. Only 13 aircraft actually off as W/C Marchbanks aircraft swung on take off forcing the Pilot to cut the engines to avoid the Control Tower (only 75 yards from the runway). The undercarriage collapsed and the aircraft caught fire. The Pilot received slight facial injuries and the Navigator fell badly evacuating the aircraft but was not seriously injured. The Air Commodore later thanked the fire party for their prompt and efficient response.

One aircraft was forced to jettison south of Berlin due to engine failure. This attack appeared to be well concentrated but was only partially successful. Flak not as heavy as expected. Searchlights numerous. Many night fighters seen but no combats.

One aircraft failed to return.

JD 407 (R)

Sgt. Roadley Killed.
Sgt. Jennings Killed.
Sgt. Chalkley Killed.
Sgt. Webb Killed.
Sgt. Kirk Killed.
Sgt. Woodrow Killed.
Sgt. Roberts Killed.

25th August, 1943

Body of Sgt. Roadley missing from operations on the night of the 23rd-24th August picked up 100 miles south east of Norfolk. Body taken to Coltishall.

Ruhr Valley Express
IPW Copyright

27th-28th August, 1943

Nuremburg. 17 aircraft. One returned early with engine failure and one was forced to jettison south of Luxemburg due to glycol leak. Due to several factors this raid was not a success. Night fighters active. 2 aircraft had combats and one claimed to have destroyed a night fighter. The Navigator of another aircraft Sgt. Hague was killed by flak over Mannheim. This aircraft was forced to make an emergency landing at Tangmere. Light flak. Numerous searchlights.

On return all aircraft were diverted due to weather.
One aircraft failed to return.
JB 835 (X)

F/S Sproat Killed.
Sgt. Gold Killed.
Sgt. Firth Killed.
Sgt. Painter Killed.

Sgt. Horten Prisoner of War.
Sgt. Gauntlett Killed.
Sgt. Rees Killed.

29th August, 1943

Due to bad visibility and cross wind one aircraft swung and collapsed undercarriage in "Watch Tower Protection Trap" (Ditch). This had now caused the loss of 5 aircraft.

30th-31st August, 1943

Munchen Gladbach. 13 aircraft. One returned early due to failure of air bomber's oxygen supply. Well concentrated attack with fires gaining a good hold towards the end. Night fighters active. 2 aircraft had combats and one Rear Gunner of one was wounded. One other aircraft was also damaged by a 3 second burst from another Halifax.

One aircraft failed to return.

JD 128 (M)

F/S Chappell Killed.
Sgt. Lee Killed.
F/O Smallfield Killed.
F/S Zander Killed.
Sgt. Smart Killed.
Sgt. Harris Killed.
Sgt. Jones Killed.

31st August-1st September, 1943

Berlin. 10 aircraft. This attack lasted only 29 minutes and consisted of 621 aircraft in 6 waves. Crews thought bombing well concentrated but it was in fact scattered and short of the target. Flak light over target. Numerous night fighters.

One aircraft failed to return.

JN 909 (B)

Sgt. Rowbottom Killed.
Sgt. Keele Killed.
Sgt. Pearce Killed.
F/S Collins Prisoner of War.
F/S McClay Killed.
Sgt. Day Killed.
Sgt. Wallace Evaded capture and reached Switzerland.

4th September, 1943

2 aircraft engaged in sea search. Nothing found.

5th-6th September, 1943

Mannheim. 11 aircraft. 2 returned early one with a glycol leak and the other with Gee and Monica unserviceable and one jettisoned near Rheims due to overload tank unserviceable. This attack consisted of 6 waves lasting 34 minutes. Huge explosions seen and catastrophic damage done. Flak moderate. Searchlights numerous but ineffective. Many night fighters seen and one aircraft had an inconclusive combat.

6th-7th September, 1943

Munich. 10 aircraft. 3 returned early one with Gee and Monica unserviceable. The other 2 with unserviceable constant speed units. Marking not effective and bombing scattered. Flak negligible. Searchlights ineffective but night fighters active. One aircraft was badly damaged by a JU 88 but claimed to have shot it down and one also claimed an unidentified night fighter.

One aircraft failed to return.

JB 921

F/O Atkinson Prisoner of War. (Wounded).
F/O Butcher Prisoner of War.
Sgt. Kirkby Prisoner of War.
Sgt. Ridley Killed.
P/O Brown Killed.
Sgt. Cockroft Killed.
Sgt. Moore Prisoner of War.

The whole Bomber Force, consisting of 257 Lancasters and 147 Halifaxes flew low over London on the way out to raise civilian morale. 3 Lancasters and 13 Halifaxes did not come back.

15th-16th September, 1943

Montlucon. 12 aircraft. One returned early with compass unserviceable. This was an accurate attack and the main target (Dunlop Factory) was badly hit. Large fires were started with smoke rising to 10 000 ft. Opposition light. Flak and fighters almost non existent.

16th-17th September, 1943

Modane. 15 aircraft. One returned early unable to climb due to icing and also with electrical system unserviceable. Weather bad en route with icing and heavy cloud to 17 000 ft. Clear over target but Pathfinder markers 2 000 yards off. This attack was not successful. Opposition slight. No flak or night fighters.

On return one aircraft crashed on Garrowby Hill, north of Pocklington killing the bomb aimer Sgt. Jones and injuring the rest of the crew.

17th September, 1943

W/C S.J. Marchbank D.F.C. took Command of No 102 Squadron in place of W/C F.R.C. Fowle.

18th September, 1943

3 Russian Officers visited the Station together with their interpreter. Stayed until the 20th September, 1943.

22nd-23rd September, 1943

Hannover. 14 aircraft. Raid was considered to be a good one but strong cross winds caused most of the damage to be situated to the south east of the city. Flak negligible. Searchlights numerous but ineffective. Night fighters active. One aircraft had an inconclusive combat and one aircraft returned on 3 engines.

One aircraft failed to return.

HX 154 (K)

F/O Hanby Prisoner of War.
P/O Williams Prisoner of War.
Sgt. Taylor Prisoner of War.
Sgt. Maund Prisoner of War.
F/S Windmill Prisoner of War.
Sgt. Edlin Prisoner of War.
Sgt. Anderton Prisoner of War.

23rd-24th September, 1943

Mannheim. 12 aircraft. 2 returned early one due to sickness of a crew member and the other was unable to maintain height. Weather clear at target and 4-8/10 cloud en route. This attack was concentrated on the northern half of the target which had not been hit on the raid of the 5th-6th September, 1943.

There was a "spoof" attack on Darmstadt but this was not successful in drawing off the night fighters which were active over the target. One aircraft was attacked by a JU 88 but suffered no damage.

Flak was moderate en route but heavy at the target.

27th-28th September, 1943

Hannover. 18 aircraft. 2 returned early. One due to sickness of a crew member and the other with an unserviceable A.S.I. Weather good and Pathfinder markers clearly seen but these were not correctly placed. This resulted in the bombing being well concentrated but in open country to the north of the target.

Flak moderate to light. Night fighters active and 2 aircraft had inconclusive combats.

28th-29th September, 1943

Bullseye exercise scheduled but was cancelled due to weather.

29th-30th September, 1943

Bochum. 12 aircraft. One returned early due to engine trouble and one had to jettison owing to navigational difficulties. This attack worked perfectly and considerable damage was done.

No night fighters seen, flak and searchlights surprisingly light for the Ruhr.

1st October, 1943

One aircraft crashed after stalling and bouncing heavily when landing at Elvington.

2nd October, 1943

Blood transfusion unit visited Station. 200 volunteers.

2nd-3rd October, 1943

The Baltic. (Minelaying). 7 aircraft. One brought mines back owing to flak damage. The rest were successful. Defences slight. Heavy flak at coast.

3rd October, 1943

One aircraft crashed and burnt south east of Pocklington due to the pilot retracting the flaps too early. No injuries.

3rd-4th October, 1943

Kassel. 15 aircraft. The main weight of this attack fell on outlying areas to the west of the target but nevertheless considerable damage was done. Opposition slight.
On return, V Victor flown by F/S McPhail had the port inner engine fall off while in circuit. This damaged the propeller of the port outer engine, but the pilot carried out a brilliant 2 engined landing for which he was awarded an immediate D.F.M. (Though this is recorded in the Station Operations Record Book as an "Unusual Incident" the Squadron O.R.B. merely records that the aircraft landed at 01.21).

What is strongly believed to be a propeller blade from this aircraft together with several photographs can be seen in the Wolds Gliding Club Clubhouse.

One aircraft was also damaged by incendiaries dropped by another aircraft.

4th-5th October, 1943

Frankfurt. 14 aircraft. 6 returned early. 2 had engine trouble, one due to confusion of instructions, one with Gee unserviceable, one with overload pump unserviceable and one with unserviceable constant speed unit. Good concentration of bombs round flares which were accurately placed. Extensive damage caused.

Flak moderate and only a few fighters seen.

7th-8th October, 1943

Hanstead. (Minelaying). 5 aircraft. All successful, some heavy flak.

Loading H.E's and incendary   *IWM Copyright*

8th-9th October, 1943

Hannover. 10 aircraft. The initial reports of this raid looked good and it turned out to be what was probably the most effective attack on Hannover of the whole war.

Flak was moderate to heavy over the target. Searchlights numerous but ineffective and night fighters not as active as usual. One aircraft failed to return.

HR 927 (N)

F/S Ellis Killed.
Sgt. Rowlatt Prisoner of War.
Sgt. Woollerton Prisoner of War.
Sgt. Buchanan Prisoner of War.
Sgt. Williams Killed.

Sgt. Mason Prisoner of War.
Sgt. Palgrave Killed.

20th October, 1943

Aircraft landing after cross country flight overshot into ditch collapsing undercarriage.

22nd-23rd October, 1943

Kassel. 19 aircraft. Weather bad en route but cleared 40 miles from the target, but one aircraft was forced to jettison and return with Gee unserviceable and another with starboard outer unserviceable due to icing. The markers were accurately placed and this attack carried out by 569 aircraft over a 16 minute period was one of the most devastating of the whole war.

Flak and searchlights moderate. Numerous night fighters seen and one aircraft nearly collided with another which was taking violent evasive action. "Spoof" attack carried out on Frankfurt.

2 aircraft failed to return.

HR 911 (L)	JN 908 (Z)
P/O Brookes Killed.	F/L Kelly Prisoner of War.
Sgt. Sykes Killed.	F/S Crump Prisoner of War.
Sgt. Sewell Killed.	P/O Pell Prisoner of War.
F/S Spencer Killed.	F/S Cosford Prisoner of War.
S/L Abels (B Flight Commander) Prisoner of War	F/O Wroughton Prisoner of War.
P/O Walton Prisoner of War.	Sgt. McCarthy Prisoner of War.
Sgt. Faultey Prisoner of War.	Sgt. Jerrod Prisoner of War.
	Sgt. Fowler Killed.

3rd-4th November, 1943

Dusseldorf. 18 aircraft. Well concentrated attack with the main weight falling in the centre and south west of the city.

Flak moderate, searchlights numerous but not troublesome and only a few night fighters seen but several aircraft reported near collisions with other aircraft en route and over the target.

One aircraft had a direct hit in the fuelage causing a fire which the crew were able to extinguish, the pilot S/L Milison was forced to fly for 20 minutes without instruments owing to the dense smoke. This aircraft returned on 3 engines.

11th-12th November, 1943

Frisian Islands (Minelaying). 5 aircraft. Successful operation. All aircraft diverted on return due to weather.

One aircraft HX 157(0) failed to return. This aircraft put out an S.O.S. but as the aircraft was out of reach of our own rescue services an International Broadcast was made. Two minutes later this was acknowledged by a German Station. The crew F/S Cambell, F/L Dinglee, F/S Dyson, Sgt. Healy, Sgt. Thawl, Sgt. Yorke and Sgt. Arrowsmith were not found.

Cannes. 5 aircraft. Attack well concentrated but the target (Railway Yards and Workshops) suffered only minor damage. Opposition light.

17th November, 1943

One aircraft in sea search. Nothing found.

18th November, 1943

One aircraft swung on take off collapsing undercarriage.

18th-19th November, 1943

Ludwigshaven. 20 aircraft. Crews had to wait for target indicators as winds not as forecast. The markers were scattered resulting in the majority of the attack falling to the north of the city.

Searchlights numerous and flak moderate. Night fighters active and one aircraft claimed to have shot down a JU 88. The bombs of one aircraft were found to be "hung up" on return due to icing.

19th-20th November, 1943

Leverkusen. 14 aircraft. One returned early due to illness of crew member and Gee unserviceable. Wind not as forecast. 10/10 cloud over the target with tops to 10-12 000 ft. resulting in a badly scattered attack.

Flak intense but searchlights ineffective due to weather. Night fighters not numerous but one aircraft claimed one JU 88 shot down and another damaged.

Navigator of one aircraft Sgt. Cannock wounded by flak and another overshot into ditch on return, collapsing undercarriage.

22nd-23rd November, 1943

Berlin. 24 aircraft. 7 returned early due to various causes. Oxygen trouble, engine failure, icing and difficulties with navigation equipment. In spite of the weather, 10/10 cloud with tops to 10,000 ft. the ground markers could just be seen and this attack became the most devastating attack on Berlin of the whole war. It is described in the Operations Record Books as "a remarkable prang".

On return one aircraft collided with a No 77 Squadron (Elvington) aircraft killing both crews. Sgt. Cottle, P/O Hughes,Sgts. Babner, Bainbridge, Boxall, Dunn and F/S Wellington of No 102 Squadron and F/S Lineham, F/S Godson, Sgts. West, Tweddle, Elder, Bennett and Thompson of No 77 Squadron.

25th-26th November, 1943

Frankfurt. 22 aircraft. One returned early due to sickness of a crew member. 14 aircraft were detailed to act as Pathfinder Support and bomb blind using H2S. Results difficult to assess and later found to be scattered but a German Broadcast admitted "A heavy attack".

The aircraft which returned early crashed at Water Priory near Garrowby Hill, north of Pocklington. The pilot Sgt. Symonds the engineer Sgt. Buckle and one gunner Sgt. Jones were killed. One aircraft also hit the fence taking off, this punctured the tyre but the pilot managed to keep control on landing. One aircraft also had a bomb "hang up" which fell out on the runway on return.

2 aircraft failed to return.

HR 811 (C)   JD 366 (V)

F/L Phillips Prisoner of War.   Sgt. Pearson Killed.
F/O McPherson Killed.   Sgt. Durrant Killed.
Sgt. Lyall Killed.   Sgt. James Killed.
Sgt. Raine Prisoner of War.   Sgt. Adams Killed.
Sgt. Briant Prisoner of War.   Sgt. Addison Killed.
Sgt. Duncan Prisoner of War.   Sgt. Shore-Marston Killed.
F/S Lee Prisoner of War.   Sgt. Haddow Killed.
F/O Bolton Prisoner of War.

26th-27th November, 1943

Stuttgart. 17 aircraft. (This was a diversion for an attack on Berlin by a force of 447 Lancasters and 10 Mosquitoes). 4 aircraft were not ready after the previous nights operations. One returned early having bombed Hanau after an attack by a night fighter had shot aircraft to ribbons and killed the mid upper gunner Sgt. Peterson.

This attack was scattered and the opposition was ineffective.

3rd-4th December, 1943

Leipzig. 20 aircraft. 3 returned early, 2 with engine failure and one with Gee unserviceable. In spite of 10/10 cloud to 8 000 ft. aircraft were able to bomb on glow of green target indicators through cloud.

This attack was probably the most successful raid on this target of the whole war through crews had very little of interest to report as Pocklington aircraft bombed early in the attack.

One aircraft failed to return.

JD 303 (S)

F/O Key Killed.
F/O Tippens Prisoner of War.
Sgt. Phillips Killed.
Sgt. Cox Killed.
F/S Argent Killed.
F/O Jackson Killed.
Sgt. Guy Prisoner of War.

20th-21st December, 1943

Frankfurt. 21 aircraft. 2 returned early, one with engine trouble and the other with unserviceable hydraulics. One aircraft bombed Mannheim. This attack was scattered though considerable damage was caused.

Many dummy target indicators seen and numerous combats with night fighters observed. Flak moderate to light. Searchlights ineffective.

One aircraft failed to return.

JD 467 (R)

F/S Fiddes Killed.
Sgt. Hoynes Killed.
Sgt. Williams Killed.
Sgt. Adams Prisoner of War.
Sgt. Currie Prisoner of War.
Sgt. Kitchener Killed.
Sgt. Dunger Killed.

22nd December, 1943

One aircraft crashed taking off on engine test. No casualties.

24th-25th December, 1943

Frisian Islands. (Minelaying). 9 aircraft. All successful.

29th-30th December, 1943

Berlin. 23 aircraft. 3 returned early, one with sick crew member and the other 2 with engine trouble. 10/10 cloud over the target, to 8 000 ft. but heavy flak barrage in spite of this.

This attack well concentrated round the sky markers but these were not accurately placed resulting in bombs falling to the south and east of the city.

2 aircraft failed to return.

HR 867 (A)

P/O Fraser Prisoner of War.
F/O Hesketh Prisoner of War.
Sgt. Day Prisoner of War.
F/S Pearce Prisoner of War.
F/S O'Hare Killed.
Sgt. Mundy Prisoner of War.
Sgt. MacWhinnie Prisoner of War.
F/O Carlson Prisoner of War.

JD 412 (X)

Sgt. Stokes Killed.
Sgt. Parr Prisoner of War.
Sgt. Habberly Prisoner of War.
Sgt. Rickets Prisoner of War.
Sgt. Thompson Prisoner of War.
Sgt. Hatton Prisoner of War.
F/S Bretherton Prisoner of War.

At the end of the Runway,
The W.A.A.F. Corporal Lingers
Nervously Threading
A Scarf through her fingers

Husband? or Lover?
Or Friend for a night
Her face doesn't tell
In the dim evening light

The Squadron is airborne,
But still the W.A.A.F. Lingers
Nervously Threading
A Scarf through her fingers.

Ronald A.M. Ranson.

1944

Though Bomber Command had sustained very heavy losses in the "Battle of Berlin" the war was progressing well on all fronts.

German resistance in Italy was still strong but it was obvious that a landing in France would not long be delayed. The massive American build up in the Pacific was now showing fruit and the slow advance across the Pacific continued but at a heavy price. Burma had largely been recaptured, but again losses were heavy.

Germany was now subject to continuous air raids. The R.A.F. by night and the Americans by day, but by the end of 1944 the R.A.F. was able to operate in daylight as well. Bomber Command suffered its worse loss in the war however when 95 aircraft were lost attacking Nuremburg in April. The Germans retaliated with the V.1 and V.2 weapons which caused considerable damage but by March 1945 all the launching sites had been overrun.

The high point of 1944 was of course D Day on June 6th. In what is probably the largest military operation ever, 155 000 men were landed in 24 hours.

5th January, 1944

Brazilian Mission visited the Station.

5th-6th January, 1944

Kattegat. (Minelaying). Operation cancelled due to weather.

6th-7th January, 1944

Ile Di Die. (Minelaying). 10 aircraft. Successful operation.

8th-9th January, 1944

Limoges. Operation cancelled due to weather.

11th January, 1944

Chinese Goodwill Mission visited the Station.

20th-21st January, 1944

Berlin. 16 aircraft. One returned early with engine trouble. The result of this raid is a mystery. Everything went according to plan but no trace of this raid can be found in the German records. No reconnaissance was done until after 4 further raids. It is not therefore known whether this raid was concealed by the German authorities or the entire attack missed Berlin.

On return one aircraft, short of fuel due to flak damage, crashed near Hethel killing the Bomb Aimer F/O Turnbull and injuring the rest of the crew.

The crew of one other aircraft baled out on the Station Commander's order as they had only 5 minutes of fuel left, also due to flak damage. This aircraft crashed near Driffield.

5 aircraft failed to return.

JN 981 (N)

F/S Render Prisoner of War.
F/S Dobson Killed.
Sgt. Mowbrat Killed.
Sgt. Gover Killed.
F/O Richardson Killed.
Sgt. Lyons Killed.
Sgt. Franrish Killed.

HX 187 (H)

P/O Dean Prisoner of War.
Sgt. Stone Prisoner of War.
Sgt. Veale Prisoner of War.
F/O Lauder Killed.
F/O Nelson Killed.
F/S Towler Prisoner of War.
Sgt. Watson Killed.
Sgt. Whittle Prisoner of War.

LW 227 (X)

W/O Wilding Prisoner of War.
Sgt. Chandler Prisoner of War.
Sgt. Buxton Prisoner of War.
Sgt. Corrigan Prisoner of War.
Sgt. Heap Prisoner of War.
W/O Yeager Prisoner of War.
Sgt. Sheppard Prisoner of War.

LW 337 (F)

F/O Griffiths Prisoner of War.
F/S Wilson Prisoner of War.
F/S Church Killed.
Sgt. Brenner Killed.
F/O Underwood Prisoner of War.
F/S Dupulers Killed.
Sgt. Bushell Prisoner of War.
Sgt. Stainbridge Killed.

LW 337 (F)

F/S Compston Prisoner of War.
Sgt. Evans Prisoner of War.
Sgt. Eastwood Prisoner of War.
Sgt. Courtney Prisoner of War.
Sgt. Moss Killed.
Sgt. Smith Killed.
Sgt. Metcalfe Killed.

A Minelaying operation to Kiel Bay was cancelled due to weather.

21st-22nd January, 1944

Magdeburg. 15 aircraft. One returned early due to boost guage and rear turret unserviceable.

4 aircraft failed to return.

LW 274 (R)

Sgt. Smith Killed.
F/O Clogg Killed.
Sgt. Foster Killed.
Sgt. Belts Killed.
F/O O'Neill Killed.
Sgt. Chadwick Killed.
Sgt. Taylor Killed.

JN 952 (L)

W/O Headley Killed.
W/O Watt Prisoner of War.
Sgt. White Prisoner of War.
Sgt. Boland Killed.
F/O Nelson Killed.
F/S Plain Killed.
Sgt. Stanley Killed.

HX 150 (M)

F/S Ellis Killed.
F/O Payne Prisoner of War.
Sgt. Adams Prisoner of War.
Sgt. Symcox Killed.
F/S Millan Prisoner of War.
Sgt. Fraser Killed.
Sgt. Wilson Killed.

HX 149 (J)

F/S Gregory Prisoner of War.
F/O Bradshaw Prisoner of War.
Sgt. Mitchell Killed.
Sgt. Davies Killed.
Sgt. Irvine Prisoner of War
Sgt. Crossfield Killed.
Sgt. Bellamy Prisoner of War.

Kiel Bay. (Minelaying). Cancelled due to weather.

The last 2 nights operations were the worst of the war for casualties from Pocklington. Of 31 aircraft to operate 11 had been lost. For this raid a force of 421 Lancasters, 244 Halifaxes and three Mosquitoes had been dispatched. 22 Lancasters and 35 Halifaxes did not return. The Halifax loss rate was 15.6%.

23rd January, 1944

First performance of "Journey's End" in Station Theatre by Station Theatre Company.

25th-26th January, 1944

Bombing operation to Frankfurt cancelled.

27th January, 1944

Funeral of F/O Turnbull killed on the 21st January 1944 held at Pocklington.

27th-28th January, 1944

Bombing operation to Berlin cancelled.

28th-29th January, 1944

Berlin. 17 aircraft. 7 returned early 6 due to heavy icing raising fuel consumption to a point where it would not have been possible to reach the target and return. The seventh, with a sick wireless operator jettisoned their bombs on Sylt and returned. This completed their operational tour.

One aircraft ditched off the east coast of Scotland. The survivors were picked three days later. Though the ditching had been a success all the crew boarding the dingy, the sea later increased and a 20 ft wave threw them all out. Sgts Burgess, Purkiss and Campbell were unable to climb back in and the cold was so intense that the others could not help them and they drifted away.

Owing to the cold the surviving 4 could not open their emergency rations or fire their distress flares, although they could see aircraft searching for them. One even dropped an airborne lifeboat but they were unable to board it.

The 4 survivors were picked up by an M.T.B. but F/S Graham died on the way to hospital. The remaining 3 F/S Pugh, Sgt. Cohen and Sgt. Williams all suffered badly from exposure.

One other aircraft failed to return.

LW 277 (Y)

P/O Linsell Prisoner of War.
P/O Connelly Prisoner of War.
Sgt. Cullis Prisoner of War.
Sgt. Hammond Killed.
Sgt. Godavoy Prisoner of War.
Sgt. Cowen Prisoner of War.
W/O Scott Prisoner of War.
Sgt. Ward Prisoner of War.

29th January, 1944

Sea search by 4 aircraft. Nothing found.

"Grand Circle" method of Air Traffic Control bought into use. On return all aircraft flew a large circle round Pocklington, Melbourne and Elvington calling "passing Pocklington" as they did so. This was flown as high as possible. Each aircraft was then in turn called to descend into it's individual circuit. By using this method it was possible to land 60 aircraft in 20 minutes.

2nd-3rd February, 1944

Kiel Bay. (Minelaying). 10 aircraft. 4 bought mines back as H2S unserviceable. The rest were successful.

3rd-4th February, 1944

St. Nazaire. (Minelaying). 8 aircraft. All successful.

5th-6th February, 1944

Oslo Fiord. (Minelaying). 8 aircraft. This was a very difficult operation as dropping point was a narrow channel surrounded by islands and sandbanks. H2S of no value so drop had to be visual from a low altitude. 6 were successful.

Some opposition from one light flak gun. Mid upper gunner of one aircraft fired back whereupon gun ceased firing and a small fire started which had grown quite large by the time the aircraft left.

8th February, 1944

Halifax from 1663 HCU Rufforth swung off runway on 3 engined landing collapsing undercarriage.

11th-12th February, 1944

St. Nazaire. (Minelaying). 5 aircraft. All laid mines successfully by use of H2S. 4 mines carried by each aircraft instead of the usual 2. This did not effect the performance of the aircraft though it was not possible to close the bomb doors.

12th-13th February, 1944

Frisian Islands. (Minelaying). 6 aircraft. All successful.

15th-16th February, 1944

Berlin. 20 aircraft. 7 returned early. The high number of early returns was due to technical trouble. 3 aircraft had their Gee sets go unserviceable, 3 had their overload tanks fail to feed and one had its A.S.I. iced up and one also had its incendiaries set on fire by flak and was forced to jettison and return home.

Low cloud over the Continent. Crews reported attack well concentrated and extensive damage done. Heavy flak at target. Mosquito aircraft later found pall of smoke to 20 000 ft. over the target. Cloud hampered night fighters, few were seen.

On return one aircraft hit a tree while waiting it's turn to land at Leconfield due to wrong altimeter setting. Forced to feather one engine but landed without further damage.

2 aircraft failed to return.

LW 339 (F)

F/L Hilton Killed.
F/S Paige Killed.
Sgt. Carr Killed.
Sgt. Paskell Killed.
Sgt. Dean Killed.
Sgt. Gosling Prisoner of War.
W/O Sykes Killed.

HX 155 (Q)

P/O Kularatne Killed.
Sgt. Whittaker Killed.
F/S Johnson Killed.
P/O Downs Killed.
Sgt. Stapleton Killed.
F/O Filmer Killed.
Sgt. Sherlock Killed.
P/O Manser Killed.

18th February, 1944

First issue of Pocka Gen. (Station Magazine).

3 more attacks on Berlin were ordered for the nights of 16th/17th, 17th/18th and 18th/19th February, 1944 but they were cancelled.

19th-20th February, 1944

Leipzig. 19 aircraft. 4 returned early, 2 with overload tanks unserviceable and the others with engine and W.T. unserviceable. One aircraft was forced to return after the wireless operator Sgt.

Chance was wounded.

The forecast wind was wrong and the main force had to wait. Raid appeared concentrated at first but became scattered.

Many combats with night fighters. One aircraft claimed to have shot down a JU 88 and another was badly shot up by an unseen fighter.

2 aircraft failed to return.

HX 185 (B)

F/O Dean Prisoner of War.
Sgt. Trett Prisoner of War.
Sgt. Milner Prisoner of War.
P/O Stenning Prisoner of War.
Sgt. Loosemore Prisoner of War.
Sgt. Clarke Prisoner of War.
W/O Dryden Prisoner of War.

JN 972 (H)

F/S Cummings Killed.
F/O McInerney Prisoner of War.
Sgt. Lingley Killed.
Sgt. Rees Killed.
Sgt. Torrance Killed.
Sgt. Giddings Prisoner of War.
F/S Clark Killed.

Control Tower in 1985 (claimed to be haunted)

20th-21st February, 1944

Bombing operation to Stuttgart cancelled.

21st-22nd February, 1944

St. Nazaire. (Minelaying). 5 aircraft. One brought mines back as H2S unserviceable. The rest were successful.

22nd-23rd February, 1944

Kiel Bay. (Minelaying). 11 aircraft. Recalled due to weather.

24th-25th February, 1944

Kiel Bay. (Minelaying). 13 aircraft. Pathfinder technique used for aircraft without H2S. Operation an outstanding success. 30 mines laid out of 34. One aircraft badly damaged by a night fighter but got back safely and one brought mines back, unable to determine position.

This was a diversion for a major raid on Schweinfurt by a force of 734 aircraft. This followed the daylight raid by 266 U.S.A.F. B17's the previous day.

25th-26th February, 1944

Kiel Bay (Minelaying). 13 aircraft. 3 returned early due to oxygen failure, engine trouble and icing. The rest mined successfully again using Pathfinder technique.

Two aircraft returned on 2 engines. One landed safely at Base "A fine display of airmanship". The other LW331 (D) ditched under the cover of Flamborough Head. No trace found of the crew. F/S Rodgers, W/O Lalonde, F/L Leithed, Sgt. Burns, Sgt. Brown, Sgt. Lloyd and F/S Metka.

27th February, 1944

Station Snow Clearance Plan put into operation after a 4" fall of snow. Runways serviceable again by afternoon of 28th.

The losses of Halifax Mk 2 aircraft had now reached an unacceptable level. Since the start of the year 18 No 102 Squadron aircraft had been lost out of a total of 87 despatched, a loss rate of nearly 21%. This Squadron, together other Halifax Mk 2 Squadrons was now withdrawn from operations against Germany until they could be re-equipped with the more powerful Hercules engined Halifax Mk 3's.

28th-29th February, 1944

Kiel Bay (Minelaying). Operation cancelled.

1st-2nd March, 1944

St. Nazaire. (Minelaying). Operation cancelled.

2nd-3rd March, 1944

Meulaw Les Meureaux. (Aircraft Factory). 15 aircraft. (4 crews also offered for surplus No 77 Squadron aircraft). 2 returned early one with engine failure and the other with Gee and Monica unserviceable and two were forced to jettison as no target indicators visible. The target was badly damaged, most crews obtaining an aiming point photograph. No opposition.

3rd-4th March, 1944

St. Nazaire. (Minelaying). 7 aircraft. One returned early due to engine failure. One aircraft returned with mines still on board and diverted to Woodbridge Emergency Airfield. The rest laid mines successfully.

6th-7th March, 1944

Trappes Marshalling Yard. 16 aircraft. (2 crews also supplied for surplus No 77 Squadron aircraft). 2 aircraft bombed on 3 engines. 15 aiming point photographs showed target indicators dead on target. This attack caused enormous damage to the railway yards and installations.

This was an experimental attack on a small target from a high altitude of 15 000 ft. However, most Pocklington aircraft bombed from between 9 and 12 000 ft.

7th-8th March, 1944

Le Mans Marshalling Yard. 13 aircraft. Attack took place in low cloud through which target indicators could just be seen. Not thought to have been an effective attack at the time but later found to have been successful.

2 aircraft jettisoned their bombs safe as they could not see the markers.

8th March, 1944

New production of "Diversion" by Station Concert Party.

8th-9th, 9th-10th and 10th-11th March, 1944

3 further attacks on Le Mans Marshalling Yard were ordered but cancelled due to weather.

11th-12th March, 1944

Mining operation cancelled due to weather.

**Post operations drink (usually laced with Rum) before de-briefing.
Note the signs of stress in the Pilots face.** *IWM Copyright*

13th-14th March, 1944

Le Mans Marshalling Yard. 16 aircraft. Target marked by Mosquitoes which were accurate and on time. Bombing well concentrated and good photographs obtained.

One fighter seen. Flak negligible.

15th-16th March, 1944

Amiens Marshalling Yard. 22 aircraft. One returned early on three engines. Cloud obscured target but target indicators laid by Mosquitoes visible. Believed to have been a very successful attack. Several aircraft were observed to be shot down en route to the target and several pilots commented adversely that the route lay through a searchlight belt 40 miles north of the target.

16th March, 1944

Boxing tournament held at Tadcaster. York Bomber Group versus Army.

16th-17th March, 1944

Amiens Marshalling Yard. 17 aircraft. One returned early due to engine trouble. Mosquito marking again accurate resulting in a successful attack. Aircraft routed round searchlight belt. No opposition.

17th March, 1944

Station Concert Party visited the Garrison Theatre at Leeds.

18th-19th March, 1944

Heligoland. (Minelaying). 12 aircraft. All successful.

22nd March, 1944

A.C. Clayton killed in road accident on Hull/York road.

The new Control Tower became operational. It was located on the north side of the airfield near the Barmby Moor/Pocklington road. (It was finally demolished in 1986). The old Tower was on the south side of the airfield near the long runway where it was a considerable obstruction if an aircraft should swing during take off.

22nd-23rd March, 1944

Kiel Bay. (Minelaying). 18 aircraft. Route markers were dropped by 6 Group aircraft but were not seen. 49 mines laid successfully but one aircraft had a "hang up" and bought mines back. Considerable flak activity mostly south of track.

23rd-24th March, 1944

Laon Marshalling Yard. 18 aircraft. 2 returned early with engine trouble. Owing to failure with P.F.F. equipment only 2 green target indicators were dropped. This resulted in 6 aircraft having to jettison in the sea as crews were ordered not to bomb visually.

One aircraft failed to return.

HR 978 (V)

F/S Garside Killed.
W/O Owens Killed.
Sgt. Maynard Killed.
Sgt. Smith Killed.
Sgt. Walker Killed.
Sgt. Catlow Killed.
F/O Roach Killed.

25th-26th March, 1944

Aulnoye Marshalling Yard. 10 aircraft. Bombing well concentrated round markers but these were slightly to the east of the target so most bombs fell wide.

26th-27th March, 1944

Couttrai Marshalling Yard. 16 aircraft. One returned early with engine trouble. Target accurately marked by Mosquitoes. Bombing well concentrated with one huge explosion (probably an ammunition train). No opposition but one aircraft had to land at Wittering with aileron control trouble.

30th March, 1944

Demonstration of Ploughing, Harrowing and Mechanical Cultivation given by East Riding War Agricultural Committee.

30th-31st March, 1944

Heligoland. (Minelaying). 10 aircraft. All successful. This operation was a diversion for the main force attack on Nuremburg. It was not effective, of the 795 aircraft despatched to Nuremburg 95 were lost. This was Bomber Commands heaviest losses in one night of the whole War. (It is not generally realised that on this night Bomber Command lost more men than Fighter Command did in the entire Battle of Britain)

It was announced that w.e.f. 1st March, 1944 sorties against French targets with a few exceptions would only count as 1/3 of a mission towards completing tour. "This was a most unpopular ruling as all crews are affected by it".

Though the Squadron was officially stood down it actually flew the highest number of sorties ever in one month, 177. The next highest was 158 in August, 1943.

An extra burden was the considerable amount of cross country training for the Conversion Flights, however, this extra burden was accepted and more than 50 crews were passed out.

1st-2nd April, 1944

Texel. (Minelaying). 9 aircraft. All successful but one aircraft had to divert to Woodbridge with low brake pressure. No opposition.

4th-5th April, 1944

2 minelaying operations to the Frisian Islands were cancelled due to weather.

6th-7th April, 1944

Bombing operation to the Marshalling Yards at Paris was cancelled due to weather.

7th-8th April, 1944

Frisian Islands. (Minelaying). 12 aircraft. All laid mines successfully on H2S fixes. No opposition.

A bombing operation to the Marshalling Yards at Paris with Lille as an alternative was cancelled due to weather.

8th April, 1944

G/C R.H. Russel, D.F.C took over as Station Commander from G/C North Carter D.F.C. who was posted to Air Ministry.

9th-10th April, 1944

Lille Marshalling Yard. 16 aircraft. One returned early with port outer unserviceable. Bombed through 5-8/10 cloud. Much damage caused to railway installations but many bombs fell outside the target area. Slight opposition.

10th-11th April, 1944

Tergnier Marshalling Yard. 16 aircraft. Target indicators clearly seen resulting in accurate attack in good weather. More opposition than usual for a French target. Searchlights and night fighters active. One aircraft had an inconclusive combat and one was forced to jettison due to a fire in the bomb bay.

11th-12th April, 1944

Kattegat. (Minelaying). 9 aircraft. One was forced to jettison with Gee unserviceable but the rest laid mines successfully in spite of bad weather. One aircraft slightly damaged by flak.

12th-13th April, 1944

A bombing operation to Coutrai and minelaying operations to Heligoland and St. Malo were cancelled due to weather.

13th April, 1944

Leeds Blood Transfusion Unit visited the Station. 292 donors.

15th-16th April, 1944

Mining operations to St. Malo, Cherbourg and Le Havre with 9 aircraft cancelled due to weather.

17th-18th April, 1944

Kiel Bay. (Minelaying). 12 aircraft. 2 took off and laid mines successfully but the next aircraft swung on take off collapsing undercarriage and blocking the runway. The pilot, F/L Jackson was on the last operation of his tour.

18th-19th April, 1944

Kiel Bay and Koge Bay. (Minelaying). 12 aircraft. All laid mines successfully and also dropped flares for 3 Group Stirlings. One aircraft had mine "hang up". No opposition.

20th-21st April, 1944

Ottignes Marshalling Yard. 12 aircraft. All bombed accurately. Slight opposition.

St. Malo. (Minelaying). 4 aircraft. All successful.

21st-22nd April, 1944

Lorient. (Minelaying). 10 aircraft. All successful. 2 aircraft reported heavy accurate A.A. Fire.

22nd April, 1944

Airborne Lifeboat Demonstration held.

22nd-23rd April, 1944

Laon Marshalling Yard. 15 aircraft. All bombed accurately and severe damage done. Few enemy aircraft seen. A.A. Fire slight.

23rd-24th April, 1944

Cadet Channel (Minelaying). 14 aircraft. 7 aircraft also carried leaflets which were dropped on the west coast of Denmark. All mines laid successfully.

Accurate A.A. fire and considerable fighter activity. One aircraft (F/L McPhail) hit by A.A. fire putting intercom U/S. Then attacked by 2 night fighters but claimed one shot down and still managed to lay mines accurately.

One aircraft overshot on landing so 2 aircraft had to be diverted to Elvington.

One aircraft failed to return.

HX 151 (M)

F/O Hall Killed.
F/O Painter Killed.
Sgt. Woplin Killed.
Sgt. Loke Killed.
Sgt. Clarke Killed.
Sgt. Pearce Killed.
F/S Weir Killed.

25th-26th April, 1944

A bombing operation to Velleneuve St. Georges was cancelled due to weather.

26th-27th April, 1944

Villeneuve St. Georges Railway Yards. 17 aircraft. All attacked the primary badly damaging the railway yards. A.A. Fire slight but 2 aircraft sighted night fighters and one was attacked.

27th-28th April, 1944

Aulnoye Marshalling Yard. 16 aircraft. Successful operation. 2 fighters seen and one made inconclusive attack. One aircraft failed to return (the only loss out of the 223 aircraft engaged in this operation).

JN 948 (N)

F/L Silverdan Killed.
F/O Blake Killed.
Sgt. Webb Killed.
Sgt. Russell Killed.
Sgt. Robertson Killed.
Sgt. Collier Killed.
F/S McClelland Killed.

29th April, 1944

Lord Trenchard "The Father of the Royal Air Force" visited the Station and watched take off for minelaying operation.

29th-30th April, 1944

East Frisian Islands. 5 aircraft. Brest. 2 aircraft. Lorient. 2 aircraft. St. Nazaire. 2 aircraft. (Minelaying). One returned early on 3 engines. No night fighter activity but heavy accurate A.A. fire at Brest and Lorient.

30th April-1st May, 1944

Mouth of River Gironde. 6 aircraft. La Rochelle. 3 aircraft. (Minelaying). Clear weather. No opposition.

1st May, 1944

Station Cinema opened by A.V.M. "Gus" Walker.

1st-2nd May, 1944

Le Havre. 2 aircraft. Cherbourg. 2 aircraft. St. Malo. 2 aircraft. Merlaix. 2 aircraft. (Minelaying). All mines dropped accurately in clear weather. No opposition.

2nd May, 1944

Aircraft being ferried to Marston Moor burst a tyre on landing.

2nd-3rd May, 1944

A minelaying operation to Kiel Bay with 12 aircraft was cancelled due to weather.

4th May, 1944

Inauguration of R.A.F. Camp domestic night. To be held on first Thursday of every month.

4th-5th May, 1944

Brest, Lorient, St. Nazaire. (Minelaying). 12 aircraft. 2 returned early one due to icing and the other with H2S unserviceable. All successful. Intense accurate A.A. fire at Lorient. Weather bad, severe icing and electrical storms.

One aircraft forced to jettison with starboard outer unserviceable. This aircraft landed at Davidstow Moor short of fuel.

5th-6th April, 1944

Brest, Lorient. St. Nazaire. (Minelaying). 6 aircraft. Successful operation but one aircraft brought mines back due to icing. Accurate A.A. fire at Lorient.

6th May, 1944

Aircraft on cross country had engine fire. All the crew baled out successfully. The aircraft is reported to have crashed at Lonesome Hill. No trace can be found of this place but a Halifax aircraft did crash at Lovesome Hill between Northallerton and Great Ayton on this date.

7th May, 1944

During a demonstration of an overshoot on 3 engines with the starboard outer feathered the starboard inner failed. This aircraft crash landed in a field but there were no casualties.

9th-10th May, 1944

Texel. (Minelaying). 4 aircraft. Successful operation. No opposition.

10th-11th May, 1944

Le Havre. (Minelaying). 3 aircraft. Successful operation. No opposition.

11th May, 1944

The re-equipping of the Squadron with Halifax III aircraft commenced. (The Halifax III had Hercules Engines giving 1 580 HP each at take off at an all up weight of 65 000 lb. It compared to the 1 280 HP of the Merlin engines of the Halifax II at a weight of 60 000 lb. It was also fitted with the large "Billiard Table" fins which eliminated the "Fin Stall" at low airspeeds which had dogged the earlier Marks of halifax).

13th May, 1944

Holme on Spalding Moor Concert Party visited Station and entertained personnel.

15th May, 1944

Conversion to Halifax III aircraft completed.

15th-16th May, 1944

Heligoland Bight. (Minelaying). 5 aircraft. This was the first operation with Halifax III aircraft. One brought mines back owing to H2S failure. The rest laid mines successfully. No opposition.

21st-22nd May, 1944

Kattegat. (Minelaying). 8 aircraft. 2 returned early with H2S unserviceable. Some fighter activity and slight inaccurate A.A. fire from 2 flak ships off the west Danish coast. No fighters.

22nd-23rd May, 1944

Orleans Marshalling Yard. 9 aircraft. One returned early with special equipment unserviceable and a petrol leak. Accurate attack. Negligible opposition and one inconclusive combat.

La Rochelle. (Minelaying). 6 aircraft. One returned early due to navigational error. Rest laid mines accurately.

24th-25th May, 1944

Colline Beaumont Coastal Gun Battery. 9 aircraft. Successful attack against only slight opposition.

Brest. (Minelaying). 6 aircraft. One returned early with engine unserviceable. All successful. Slight opposition.

25th-26th May, 1944

Bombing operation on Mannheim cancelled due to weather.

27th-28th May, 1944

Bourg Leopold Military Camp. 9 aircraft. Severe damage caused. Considerable night fighter activity. Several combats observed. A.A. slight.

One aircraft failed to return.

MZ 649 (Y)

F/O Huycke Prisoner of War.
F/O Godsell Prisoner of War.
F/O Scott Prisoner of War.
F/S Collins Prisoner of War.
Sgt. Burne Killed.
Sgt. Lethbridge Killed.
Sgt. Welsh Prisoner of War.

Brest. (Minelaying). 8 aircraft. Successful operation except for one aircraft which had mines fall out when bomb doors opened. No opposition.

28th-29th May, 1944

St. Nazaire. 2 aircraft. Lorient 2 aircraft. (Minelaying). All successful but had to divert to St. Eval on return due to weather.

A minelaying operation to the Kattegat with 5 aircraft was cancelled due to weather.

29th-30th May, 1944

Brest 4 aircraft. Kattegat 5 aircraft (Minelaying). The Kattegat operation was cancelled due to weather. One aircraft returned early from the Brest operation as it was unable to pin-point position, and one bought mines back as H2S unserviceable. The remaining 2 were successful. No opposition.

All aircraft were again diverted to St. Eval on return.

31st May-1st June, 1944

Trappes Marshalling Yard. 8 aircraft. 3 returned due to getting off track in bad weather. Successful operation.

Ijmuiden 2 aircraft. St. Malo 2 aircraft. Le Havre 2 aircraft Brest 2 aircraft (Minelaying). One returned due to a thunderstorm knocking out its H2S. Rest laid mines accurately but both operations encountered severe thunderstorms.

During the Month of May 1944 No 10 Squadron at Melbourne was transferred to No. 44 Base Holme-on Spalding Moor and No. 77 Squadron was moved to Full Sutton which was attached to 41 Base Pocklington. Nos. 346 and 347 (Free French) Squadrons moved into Elvington in June/July 1944.

1st-2nd June, 1944

La Rochelle. 2 aircraft Le Havre aircraft (Minelaying). All laid mines accurately. No opposition.

2nd-3rd June, 1944

Haringzelles "Defended Locality". 16 aircraft. 4 aircraft brought their bombs back as they could see neither the target or the target indicators.

The rest were successful in spite of 10/10ths cloud. Some light flak.

This was a diversion operation to make the Germans think the invasion was to be in the Calais area.

3rd-4th June, 1944

Bombing operation to a Heavy Gun Battery at Etaples was cancelled due to weather.

Performance of "French without Tears" given by Station Concert Party.

Salute the Soldier week opened with a target of £1000

4th-5th June, 1944

Bologne. "Defended Locality". 18 aircraft. One returned early with engine trouble and one missed the target due to a navigational error. The remainder bombed successfully. Opposition light, some A.A. Fire.

5th-6th June, 1944 (D Day)

Maisy. "Heavy Coastal Battery". 26 aircraft. (A Squadron Record). All attacked the target through 3/10 cloud at 5 000 ft. No night fighters but some light flak. (On this day Bomber Command flew 1 211 sorties for the loss of 3 aircraft).

6th-7th June, 1944

St. Lo Road Junction. 15 aircraft. A highly concentrated attack from 2-3 000 ft. Numerous aiming point photographs obtained. Slight flak. Village of St. Lo was reported as "Completely Wiped Out".

Daylight by the time aircraft returned.

Lorient. 3 aircraft. St. Nazaire. 3 aircraft. (Minelaying). All laid mines accurately. Slight A.A. fire at Lorient.

8th-9th June, 1944

Alencon Marshalling Yard. 15 aircraft. All bombed in clear weather. Small amount of light flak.

On return weather at base had deteriorated to 10/10 cloud at 300 ft. visibility 800 yards. All aircraft were diverted to Catfoss which was the only airfield clear but was unable to cope with large numbers. 4 aircraft landed at Catfoss, the remainder managed to get into Lisset, Carnaby, Driffield and Dunholme Lodge with the exception of one crew who baled out successfully owing to petrol shortage north west of Catfoss after pointing the aircraft out to sea. This aircraft crashed at Wass near Catfoss.

Brest. 10 aircraft (Minelaying). Successful operation despite heavy flak at the target.

On return all aircraft were diverted and one, LW 140 (Q) crashed after hitting a tree near Catfoss killing all the crew. W/O Jekyll, F/O Lillington, F/O Hillrich, Sgt. Downe, Sgt. Roger, Sgt. Catterwell and Sgt. Florent. It was believed that this aircraft had dived another Halifax.

10th-11th June, 1944

Brest. 4 aircraft. Le Havre 4 aircraft. (Minelaying). This was a successful operation but met heavy accurate A.A. fire at Brest.

A bombing operation to an unspecified target in northern France was cancelled.

11th-12th June 1944

Massey Plaiseau. 12 aircraft. 5 aircraft bought their bombs back as they could not identify the target in the thick weather. The remaining crews did not regard this as a successful attack. One aircraft came down to 2, 000 ft. Moderate to heavy flak at the target and one aircraft had a combat with a single engined night fighter.

One aircraft failed to return.

MZ 651 (Z)

F/S Singleton Killed.
Sgt. Thomas Killed.
F/S McNamara Killed.
F/S Robson Killed.

Sgt. Lishman Killed.
Sgt. Francis Killed.
Sgt. Smith Killed.

149

Brest. 3 aircraft. Le Havre 6 aircraft. (Minelaying). All laid mines as ordered. Heavy A.A. fire at Brest but only light opposition at Le Havre.

14th June, 1944

Funeral of Sgt. Florent killed on 9th June, held at Pocklington.

14th-15th June, 1944

Evercy. (Troop Positions). 21 aircraft. One missed the target owing to large navigational error. Reports and photographs showed this to have been a highly successful operation. Slight flak and one inconclusive combat.

Due to several factors, confusion of orders, intercom, navigational aids W.T. and both turrets being unserviceable the navigator of one aircraft Sgt. Harris baled out over the target but managed to return to the Squadron a few days later.

15th June, 1944

A bombing operation to an unspecified target in northern France with 22 aircraft was cancelled at 16.00 hours.

W/C L.D. Wilson D.F.C. A.F.C. took Command of No 102 Squadron. Salute the Soldier Week ended. The target was £1 000 but in fact £2,100 was raised.

16th-17th June, 1944

Sterkrade Oil Plant. 23 aircraft. 2 returned early with engine trouble. Bombing scattered as markers could only be dimly seen through thick cloud.

The route to the target lay over a German Night Fighter Beacon at Bocholt only 30 miles from the target which was being used as a holding point. This resulted in considerable night fighter activity from the target to the coast. There was also considerable A.A. Fire. Of the 321 aircraft despatched on this operation, 31 were lost.

5 aircraft failed to return.

MZ 301 (M)

S/L Fisher (B. Flight Commander) Killed.
F/O Striowski Killed.
P/O Buglass Killed.

MZ 292 (C)

F/S Kelso Killed.
Sgt. Gibson Killed.
Sgt. Hill Killed.

F/O Watts Killed.
F/L Cook Killed.
Sgt. Parker Killed.
Sgt. Clough Killed.

MZ 642 (O)

Sgt. Barr Killed.
Sgt. Tweed Prisoner of War.
F/S Duggleby Killed.
Sgt. Wakeford Killed.
Sgt. Chapman Prisoner of War.
Sgt. Bowman Killed.
Sgt. Bender Killed.

MZ 652 (Z)

F/O Maxwell Killed.
F/O Rushforth Killed.
Sgt. Peel Killed.
Sgt. Stamper Killed.
Sgt. Amstein Killed.
Sgt. McKenna Killed.
Sgt. Walker Killed.

Sgt. Batram Killed.
Sgt. Howarth Killed.
Sgt. Jennings Killed.
Sgt. Smith Killed.

LW 192 (R)

F/S Braddock Killed.
Sgt. Reid Killed.
Sgt. Putt Killed.
Sgt. Booker Killed.
Sgt. Finch Killed.
Sgt. Hadfield Killed.
Sgt. Zaccheo Killed.

This was the worst night for losses from Pocklington since the night of January 20th-21st. However, No 77 Squadron at Full Sutton lost 7 aircraft out of 23.

17th-18th June, 1944

An operation to an unspecified target in northern France with 16 aircraft was cancelled due to weather.

18th-19th June, 1944

Mod Ski Sitel V.1 Site. 18 aircraft. Cancelled due to weather.

19th-20th June, 1944

Domleger V.1 Site. 19 aircraft. Recalled when the weather deteriorated.

20th June, 1944

Daylight operation cancelled due to weather.

20th-21st June, 1944

An operation to an unspecified target in northern France was cancelled due to weather.

21st June, 1944

Renescure. V.1 Site. 21 aircraft. Cancelled due to weather.

22nd-23rd June, 1944

Laon Marshalling Yard. 15 aircraft. All attacked the target successfully. Flak negligible but night fighters active. 4 aircraft had combats, 2 were damaged and the rear gunner of one was wounded, but carried on firing.

Brest. (Minelaying). 6 aircraft. All laid mines in spite of heavy flak.

24th June, 1944

Noyelle En Chaussle V.1 Site. 20 aircraft. This daylight operation with fighter escort was the first from Pocklington since an abortive attack on Hamburg on the 3rd August, 1942. All bombed the target but one was forced to jettison after partial "hang up". Target indicators clearly seen.

Heavy predicted flak over Abbeville damaged 3 aircraft wounding the pilot and flight engineer of one. This aircraft landed at Ford.

25th June, 1944

Montorgueil V.1 Site. 18 aircraft. All bombed successfully but one had partial "hang up" over the target. Heavy flak over the target and one aircraft seen to explode. This aircraft was believed to have been hit by the bombs from another aircraft. Fighter escort.

On return one aircraft overshot due to bad visibility. No casualties.

One aircraft failed to return.

MZ 753 (M)
S/L Treasure Killed (B Flight Commander).
F/O Bailey Killed.
F/O Fraser Killed.
Sgt. Collins Killed.
Sgt. Archard Killed.
Sgt. Bland Killed.
Sgt. Sykes Killed.

26th June, 1944

Cormette V.1 Site. 18 aircraft. Cancelled due to weather.

26th-27th June, 1944

An attack on an unspecified target in northern France was cancelled due to weather.

27th June, 1944

Cormette V.1 Site. 20 aircraft. Cancelled due to weather.

27th-28th June, 1944

Mont Candon V.1 Site. 17 aircraft. All bombed on well concentrated markers but later photographs showed main area of attack to the east of the target.

Light flak at the target and on the way back but no fighters.

28th June, 1944

Station Concert Party presented "Music Box Revue".

28th-29th June, 1944

Blainville Marshalling Yard. 20 aircraft. 2 returned early one due to engine and compass unserviceable and the other was late taking off. Master Bomber clearly heard and instructions carried out. All crews reported a successful attack but photographs showed bombing somewhat scattered.

Slight flak and night fighters numerous. 2 inconclusive combats.

5 aircraft failed to return.

LW 143 (O)

F/S Campbell Killed.
F/S Eagle Prisoner of War.
F/S Wilson Killed.
F/S Pardon Killed.
Sgt. Leverington Prisoner of War.
Sgt. Joyce Prisoner of War.
Sgt. Leslie Prisoner of War.

LW 159 (Q)

P/O Rogers Killed.
F/S Williams Prisoner of War.
W/O Wilson Killed.
F/S Ligerwood Killed.
P/O Potter Killed.
Sgt. Frost Killed.

NA 502 (S)

P/O Mulvaney Evaded Capture.
Sgt. Miller Evaded Capture.
F/S Duell Killed.
F/S Whellum Prisoner of War.
F/O Heath Evaded Capture.
F/S Bastick Evaded Capture.
Sgt. Smith Killed.

MZ 644 (V)

Sgt. Jardine Killed.
Sgt. Merrill Evaded Capture.
F/O Messer Killed.
Sgt. Crayden Evaded Capture.
Sgt. White Killed.
Sgt. Waugh Evaded Capture.
Sgt. Dales Killed.

MZ 2646 (W)

Sgt. Robinson Killed.
Sgt. Watkins Prisoner of War.
Sgt. Woodward Killed.
Sgt. Lucas Killed.
Sgt. Partridge Killed.
Sgt. Higman Prisoner of War.
Sgt. Fingleton Killed.

29th June, 1944

Villers L'Hopital V.1 Site. 16 aircraft. Cancelled due to weather.

30th June, 1944

St. Martin L'Hortier V.1 Site. 16 aircraft. Postponed to daylight on the 1st July, 1944

The Station strength at the end of June, 1944 was:-

	OFFICERS	NCO's & AIRMEN
R.A.F.	147	1,483
R.C.A.F.	9	11
R.A.A.F.	11	22
R.N.Z.A.F.	2	1
W.A.A.F.	11	419
TOTAL	180	1,926
	2,106	

1st July, 1944

St. Martin L'Hortier V.1 Construction Site. 15 aircraft. Bombed on "Navigational Aids" as the target was obscured by cloud. No results seen.

Small amount of heavy flak. One aircraft damaged.

Fighter escort.

2nd-3rd July, 1944

An attack to an unspecified target in northern France with 18 aircraft was cancelled due to weather.

3rd July, 1944

Domlegger V.1 Site. 18 aircraft. Cancelled due to weather.

4th July, 1944

Domlegger V.1 Site. 18 aircraft. Target identified visually and bombing well concentrated. Confirmed by photographs. Small amount of light flak in target area. One aircraft damaged and mid upper gunner slightly wounded. No fighter opposition. Fighter escort.

5th July, 1944

An attack on an unspecified target in northern France with 15 aircraft was cancelled due to weather.

6th July, 1944

Mimoyecques V.1 Construction Site. 14 aircraft. This attack took place in the early morning, the first aircraft bombing at 08.17 and the last at 08.23. 1/2. the bombing was well concentrated and this was confirmed by photographs.

Heavy flak at the target and in the Calais area.

One aircraft damaged. Fighter escort.

The Master Bomber on this occasion was G/C G.L. Cheshire. It was his 100th and last operation. His first was in a 102 Squadron Whitley from Driffield on the 9th June, 1940, to bomb Abbeville Bridge.

This remarkable man has gone on to an even more outstanding peacetime career. His magnificent work for and devotion to the incurably sick is well known.

Lord Cheshire died on 31st July 1992 aged 75.

6th-7th July, 1944

Brest. (Minelaying). 6 aircraft. Cancelled due to weather.

7th July, 1944

Bremont V.1 Construction Site. 6 aircraft. Cancelled due to weather.

Caen. 15 aircraft. All attacked the primary except one who had bombs "hang up". Crews enthusiastic about effect and photographs confirmed bombing well concentrated round markers.

Considerable flak over target and enemy lines but no fighter opposition. Fighter escort.

9th-10th July, 1944

Lorient. 4 aircraft. St. Nazaire. 4 aircraft. (Minelaying). 1 returned early and landed at Weston Zoyland with engine trouble. Slight flak over Lorient.

10th July, 1944

An operation to Les Haut Buissons V.1 Site was postponed then cancelled.

12th-13th July, 1944

Les Haut Buissons V.1 Site. 19 aircraft. This attack was postponed from daylight to dark. Cloud obscured target but crews thought that if markers correctly placed this should be an effective attack and this turned out to be so.

Flak negligible. No night fighters.

15th July, 1944

W/C L.D. Wilson D.F.C. A.F.C. took Command of No 102 Squadron. Station visited by Deputy Chief of Air Staff.

Parade of Airmen and Airwomen held for "Salute the Soldier" Week in Pocklington.

15th-16th July, 1944

An attack on an unspecified target in northern France was cancelled due to weather.

16th July, 1944

Bois De La Haie V.1 Site cancelled due to weather.

17th July, 1944

Bois De La Haie V.1 Site. 21 aircraft. One returned early with engine trouble. The rest attacked visually and photographs confirmed this was a successful attack.

Slight flak but no fighter opposition. Fighter escort.

18th July, 1944

Caen. 4 aircraft. Early morning attack, the first aircraft took off at 03.46 returning at 07.43. Effective attack. Slight opposition. Fighter escort.

Vaires Marshalling Yard. 12 aircraft. Evening attack. All took off at about 15.30 and returning at about 20.15. Target easily identified visually and photographs confirm bombing well concentrated.

Moderate to heavy flak at the target. No fighter opposition. Fighter escort.

Bomb load for 'Q' Queenie - H.E's and incendiaries on bomb trolley
IWM Copyright

18th-19th July, 1944

West Frisian Islands. 4 aircraft. Heligoland Bight. 4 aircraft. (Minelaying). All laid mines successfully. Quiet trip.

19th July, 1944

Foret Du Croc V.1 Site. 14 aircraft. Cancelled due to weather.

20th July, 1944

Chapelle Notre Dame V.1 Construction Site. 14 aircraft. Markers difficult to see in haze but photographs confirm bombing well concentrated. Negligible opposition. Fighter escort.

One aircraft reported "Haze and smoke over target. Y. U/S. Fishpond U/S, port inner cutting out periodically. No oxygen to rear turret. Windscreen broken by bird. Lousy trip".

20th-21st July, 1944

Bottrup Oil Refining Plant. 9 aircraft. Cancelled due to weather.

Ardouval V.1 Site. 9 aircraft. Only 2 bombed, the rest jettisoned as no markers could be seen in dense cloud.

Opposition slight, minor damage to one aircraft and one inconclusive combat. All aircraft diverted on return.

21st July, 1944

Revilgy Sur Ornaine Railway Centre. Cancelled due to weather.

Unspecified target, cancelled due to weather.

21st-22nd July, 1944

East Frisian Islands. (Minelaying). 6 aircraft. One brought mines back owing to electrical failure. The rest successful except for one aircraft which opened fire on an unidentified enemy aircraft.

22nd July, 1944

Annual Camp for A.T.C. Cadets started.

23rd-24th July, 1944

Les Hauts Buissons V.1 Construction Site. 16 aircraft. Photographs confirm a successful attack but one aircraft had bombs "hang up" over the target.

2 aircraft had combats with night fighters and one was seen on fire in a spiral dive over the channel on the way home.

One aircraft failed to return.

MZ 298 (F)

P/O Donald Killed.
F/S Brand Killed.
F/S Lathlean Killed.
Sgt. Skeates Killed.
F/S Rogers Killed.
F/S Selth Killed.
Sgt. Cook Killed.

24th-25th July, 1944

Stuttgart. 13 aircraft. One returned early with engine trouble. Unable to reach operational height. Target covered by 10/10 cloud so aircraft were forced to bomb on flares.

Fairly intensive heavy flak at the target. Fighters active. Master Bomber jammed. One aircraft claimed to have shot down a JU 88 but sustained damage and one other aircraft had a combat with a night fighter.

One aircraft failed to return.

LL 552 (X)

F/L Page Killed.
Sgt. Simpson Killed.
Sgt. Court Killed.
Sgt. Leyland Killed.
Sgt. Ord Killed.
Sgt. Brewer Prisoner of War.
Sgt. Watkinson Killed.

25th-26th July, 1944

Wanne Eickel. 20 aircraft. One returned early with unserviceable compasses and one could not bomb owing to electrical fault so attacked alternative. The rest saw ground markers clearly but the ground was obscured by haze. Bombing was well concentrated round the markers but only a few bombs hit the prime target, the Oil Refinery.

Heavy barrage flak in target area. Night fighters active. Several combats. One aircraft which had 2 guns in mid upper turret unserviceable attacked 5 times. One claimed JU 88 as "probable".

28th July, 1944

Foret De Nieppe V.1 Construction Site. 15 aircraft. 2 returned early, one was unable to keep up and the other had navigational difficulties. The rest bombed successfully but some bombs fell short. One aircraft had its bombs fall out when the bomb doors opened.

Heavy flak over coast and at the target. No enemy aircraft. Fighter escort. One aircraft damaged by flak so jettisoned bombs on Ostend and landed at Great Ashfield with navigator F/S Spiller wounded.

28th-29th July, 1944

Foret De Nieppe V.1 Construction Site. 9 aircraft. The first of these aircraft took off at 21.58, the last of the previous raid landed at 20.22. All reported a good attack. Markers clearly seen and opposition negligible.

29th July, 1944

Foret De Chatellerault. (Fuel Dump). 21 aircraft. Cancelled due to weather.

30th July, 1944

Normandy Battle Area G. 14 aircraft. Abandoned on instruction from Master Bomber as target obscured by cloud.

On return one aircraft crashed at Eastonne near Moreton-in-the-Marsh when it struck trees attempting to land in bad weather. All the crew, F/S Hulme, F/S Riddle, F/S Jarrat, Sgt. Matthews, F/S Neilson, Sgt. Booker and Sgt. Herbert were killed.

One other aircraft was forced to land at Bury St. Edmunds due to flak damage.

30th-31st July, 1944

Foret De Chatellerault V.1 Site. 16 aircraft. Cancelled due to weather.

31st July-1st August, 1944

Further operations to Foret De Chatellerault V.1 Site. 16 aircraft. Cancelled due to weather.

1st August, 1944

Noyelle En Chausse V.1 Site. 16 aircraft. Mission abandoned on instructions from Master Bomber as there was 10/10 cloud over the target with tops to 3-4 000 ft. Crews jettisoned part of bomb load and returned to base.

Opposition slight. No enemy aircraft. Fighter escort.

2nd August, 1944

Foret De Nieppe V.1 Site. 10 aircraft. All bombed primary but photographs showed attack scattered.

Opposition slight at target but active over Ostend. No enemy aircraft. Fighter escort.

3rd August, 1944

Bois De Cassan V.1 Site. 14 aircraft. Master Bomber clearly heard, resulting in well concentrated bombing which photographs confirmed.

Slight heavy flak at target and en route. 7 aircraft slightly damaged. No fighter opposition. Fighter escort.

Foret De Nieppe V.1 Site. 10 aircraft. One was unable to identify the target but the rest carried out an accurate attack again confirmed by photographs.

Opposition slight but 2 aircraft damaged by flak. One aircraft overshot landing on return but the crew were unhurt.

5th August, 1944

Foret De Nieppe V.1 Site. 26 aircraft. One returned early with engine trouble and landed at Woodbridge. Well concentrated attack. Confirmed by photographs. One aircraft had bombs fall out when bomb doors opened and these fell across the railway line east of Hazebruck.

Fighter escort again provided. Opposition negligible.

6th August, 1944

Foret De Nieppe V.1 Site. 16 aircraft. All attacked the target and reported bombing was scattered at first but concentrated later.

Slight opposition. No enemy aircraft. Fighter escort.

7th-8th August, 1944

Totalise No. 3 (Normandy Battle Area). 12 aircraft. 11 attacked the target but smoke from the heavy concentration of bombs obscured the markers so Master Bomber cancelled operations and one aircraft brought its bombs back.

Opposition slight. No night fighters. One aircraft slightly damaged.

Brest. (Minelaying). 8 aircraft. 2 could not pinpoint the target and brought mines back as did one which had technical trouble. Rest laid mines as ordered.

Small amount of flak in target area. One aircraft damaged.

8th August, 1944

Special target in Normandy Battle zone. Cancelled.

Belle Cruix Les Bruyenes V.1 Site. 15 aircraft. A successful attack confirmed by photographs.

Heavy flak in target area damaged 2 aircraft. No fighter opposition. Fighter escort.

9th August, 1944

Foret De Mormal (Fuel Dump). 5 aircraft. Good, well concentrated attack. Large column of black smoke to 7-8 000 ft.
Opposition slight at target but Ostend and Dunkirk defences active. No fighter opposition. Fighter escort.

Halifax from 1663 H.C.U. (Rufforth) swung on landing bursting a tyre and collapsing undercarriage.

10th August, 1944

Dijon Marshalling Yard. Cancelled.
Station visited by one Officer and 25 Other Ranks from the 10th Battalion Kings Royal Rifle Corps.

11th August, 1944

Somain Marshalling Yard. 25 aircraft. One crashed on take-off following loss of power on port inner engine. Crew unhurt. In spite of ground features quickly becoming obscured by smoke and dust, a well concentrated attack was carried out.

Light flak in the Frevent and Lille area. One damaged aircraft landed at Woodbridge. No fighter opposition. Fighter escort.

12th-13th August, 1944

Russelheim (Opel Works). 9 aircraft. 2 returned early, one with engine trouble, the other with Gee unserviceable. Markers clearly seen and large fires in the target area but the Opel Works was only slightly damaged.

Heavy flak and fighters active. 2 aircraft had inconclusive combats.

One aircraft failed to return.

LW 195 (J)

F/O Sambell Prisoner of War.
Sgt. Curphly Killed.
F/S Beecroft Prisoner of War.
F/S Kidds Prisoner of War.
F/S Magill Prisoner of War.
F/S Aylmer Prisoner of War.
F/S Craig Killed.

(This was the crew that was forced to bale out on the 9th June 1944).

Brunswick. 13 aircraft. 3 returned early, one was short of fuel, the other two had engine trouble and lost time. This was an experimental raid. No Pathfinders were involved and each crew bombed using H2S. Bombing was scattered, some as much as 20 miles from the target, however a large glow of fire was seen.

Heavy barrage flak. Night fighters active. 2 aircraft had inconclusive combats.

One aircraft failed to return.

MZ 647 (R)
F/L Young Killed.
P/O Walker Killed.
Sgt. Osborne Killed.
F/S York Killed.

Sgt. Finney Killed.
F/S Gordon Killed.
F/S Harvey Killed.
Sgt. Doughty Killed.

13th August, 1944

An attack on an unspecified target was cancelled.

14th-15th August, 1944

La Rochelle. (Minelaying). 8 aircraft. One returned early with engine trouble. The rest laid mines successfully with only moderate opposition.

15th August, 1944

Eindhoven Airfield. 15 aircraft. Successful attack confirmed by photographs.

Slight flak over target but heavy at Rotterdam. Fighter escort.

This airfield was one of 8 night fighter bases to be attacked by a force of 1 004 aircraft in preparation for the coming 'winters nght' Offensive on Germany.

15th-16th August, 1944

Gironde. (Minelaying). Operation cancelled.

16th-17th August, 1944

Kiel. 15 aircraft. 2 returned early both with radar equipment unserviceable. Attack scattered but serious damage was done in the dock area.

Moderate heavy flak. Few night fighters seen.

One aircraft failed to return.

NA 504 (Y)

F/S Coughlan Killed.
F/O Pedlow Killed.
Sgt. Heal Killed.
Sgt. Townsend Killed.
Sgt. Todd Killed.
Sgt. O'Toole Killed.
Sgt. Brown Killed.

Kiel Bay. (Minelaying). 4 aircraft. Successful operation. No opposition at target but some heavy flak from Mando Island and light flak from Rumo Island. No night fighters.

River Gironde. (Minelaying). 4 aircraft. Successful operation. No opposition.

18th-19th August, 1944

Sterkade Oil Plant. 18 aircraft. 2 returned early one with engine failure and the other with an engine fire. Effective attack. 3 explosions and several large fires seen. The Oil Plant was badly damaged.

Moderate heavy and light flak at the target. Night fighters active. 6 aircraft had inconclusive combats, 2 aircraft were damaged and one claimed an ME 109 as "Damaged".

21st August, 1944

Operation to Sterkade with 15 aircraft cancelled.

22nd August, 1944

Another operation to Sterkade with 15 aircraft also cancelled.

24th August, 1944

Shipping in Brest Harbour. 14 aircraft. One returned early with air speed indicator and compasses unserviceable. 7 attacked the main target and the rest the alternative (The docks themselves). One was unable to bomb owing to an error in setting switches.

Opposition moderate but accurate. 3 aircraft damaged, one badly and 3 four engined aircraft were seen to be shot down over nearby targets.

Station visited by Sir Arthur Longmore to inspect A.T.C. Cadets.

25th August, 1944

Wemers/Capol V.1 Site. 17 aircraft. One returned early with starboard inner unserviceable. Bombing rather scattered.

Opposition slight but 3 aircraft received minor damage.

26th-27th August, 1944

An operation to Wanne Eickel Synthetic Oil Plant with 20 aircraft was cancelled.

27th August, 1944

Homberg. 19 aircraft. One returned early with unserviceable engine. All attacked the target but bad weather prevented visual operation and markers could not be seen resulting in a scattered attack.

Opposition moderate. Some heavy flak. 5 aircraft damaged. Fighter escort. "Spitfire cover worked like magic".

This raid was the first R.A.F. daylight raid on a German target, since 12th August, 1941 when a force of 54 Blenheims attacked Power Stations at Cologne for the loss of 10 aircraft.

This raid consisted of 243 aircraft. 216 Halifaxes, 13 Lancasters and 14 Mosquitoes. None were lost. Also an escort of 9 Squadrons of Spitfires was provided for the outward flight and 7 Squadrons for the return. (One ME 110 was sighted but it was driven off).

Station visited by G/C L. Wright C. of E. Assistant Chaplain in Chief who took the morning service.

28th August, 1944

Squadron detailed for an attack on Oil Tank Wagons at Givet. Operation postponed to 29th August, 1944.

29th August, 1944

Operation postponed to 30th August, 1944.

30th August, 1944

Operation cancelled at 13.10.

31st August, 1944

Lumbres Flying Bomb Site. (Though recorded as a V.1 Site this was in fact a V.2 Rocket Store). 17 aircraft. 14 attacked the target but 3 were unable to bomb as the target was obscured by cloud.

One aircraft made 4 runs before Master Bomber gave "Cease Bombing" signal. As a result, this attack was rather scattered.

No opposition at the target but heavy flak in the Watten area and one aircraft slightly damaged. No enemy aircraft seen. Fighter escort.

1st September, 1944

La Pourchinte V.2 Rocket Store. 6 aircraft. All attacked the target. Markers scattered at first but later right on aiming point. Photographs confirm this was a successful attack. Negligible opposition.

3rd September, 1944

Velno Airfield. 22 aircraft. One swung off the runway on take off, into boggy ground. No damage at the time but the tail wheel was broken by the tractor towing it clear to enable the remaining aircraft to take off.

One aircraft had bombs "hang up" but the remainder bombed markers which were right on the aiming point. (Runway intersection). Bombing well concentrated but slightly north of aiming point.

Slight to moderate flak. One Halifax seen shot down (The only loss out of 675 aircraft engaged in raids on 6 airfields). 2 aircraft were slightly damaged and one got home with 3 engines partially unserviceable. 2 engines having being stopped by flak over the target.

Aircraft diverted on return due to weather.

6th September, 1944

One aircraft returning to base after diversion to North Creake had port outer engine fail on take off. Swung off runway. No casualties. Engine failure due to water in magnetos.

6th-7th September, 1944

Frisian Islands. (Minelaying). 8 aircraft. All laid mines successfully except one which had H2S failure.

Slight opposition in the Borkum area.

9th September, 1944

Le Havre. 6 aircraft. One returned early with bombsight unserviceable. All recalled by Master Bomber as cloud obscured target when aircraft were only 2 minutes away.

One aircraft swung on landing and hit stationary aircraft. Pilot reported he could not throttle back port engine.

10th September, 1944

Le Havre. 22 aircraft. All aircraft attacked the target, gunnery defences to the north of the port, in good visibility. Large explosion at the start of the attack believed to be ammunition dump blowing up. No opposition.

11th September, 1944

Gelsenkirchen (Nordstern Synthetic Oil Plant). 17 aircraft. All bombed target in spite of smoke screen. Photographs showed good results.

Intense heavy and some light flak at the target which damaged 11 aircraft. Fighter escort.

4 Group Boxing Tournament held in aid of R.A.F. Benevolent Funds. All proceeds to fund, expenses being shared between the Stations.

12th September, 1944

Munster. (Railway Facilities). 22 aircraft. All attacked the target except one with unserviceable bomb gear. Good conditions. Bombs seen to straddle railway lines and fires started in the southern half of the city.

Flak intensive. 5 aircraft hit and one badly damaged by incendiaries from another aircraft. One aircraft landed at Woodbridge with the air bomber Sgt. N.N. Brown badly wounded. One aircraft also "Belly Landed" near Carnaby after both port engines failed.

One aircraft failed to return.

MZ 699 (T)

P/O Groves Killed.
Sgt. Munro Prisoner of War.
Sgt. Davies Prisoner of War.
W/O Paquette Prisoner of War.

Sgt. Hooker Prisoner of War.
Sgt. Duncan Killed.
Sgt. Waterman Prisoner of War

14th September, 1944

Wilhelmshaven. 16 aircraft. All took off but were recalled as the fighter escort from 11 Group could not take off due to weather.

15th-16th September, 1944

Brunsbuttel. 6 aircraft. Fehmarn Belt and Sound (Minelaying) 10 aircraft. All successful but the Brunsbuttel operation met considerable opposition. However, only one aircraft was damaged.

The mining aircraft on this operation carried mines of a type which would explode if dropped on land. All aircraft also carried four 500 lb general purpose bombs as the attack was to simulate a small raid on Brunsbuttel at the south west end of the Kaiser Wilhelm canal.

17th September, 1944

One aircraft missing following bombing practice at sea. No trace found of the crew:- Capt. Thompson (S.A.A.F.), F/S Reader, Sgt. White, W/O Locke, Sgt. Greening, Sgt. Gibson and Sgt. Aitchinson.

18th September, 1944

3 aircraft engaged in sea search for missing aircraft. Nothing found.

20th September, 1944

Calais. 13 aircraft. All attacked primary. Markers clearly seen and photographs confirm a successful attack. This raid was carried at low level, 2,500 ft. One aircraft reported it could see German troops running down the beach to the sea as the attack started. No opposition.
One aircraft landed at Grafton Underwood on three engines.

Station visited by 2 Officers and 65 other ranks of the Kings Royal Rifle Corps.

21st-22nd September, 1944

2 operations to Sterkade (Synthetic Oil Plant) with 15 aircraft cancelled.

24th September, 1944

Operation to Brussels postponed to 25th September, 1944.

25th September, 1944

22 aircraft each carrying about 750 gallons of petrol in 165 tins delivered it to Melsbroeck (Brussels). This was to alleviate the petrol shortage being experienced by allied ground forces. All arrived safely except one which diverted to Woodbridge with hydraulic trouble.

3 aircraft went unserviceable at Brussels but a party of Officers and Airmen had been sent from all 42 Base Stations to service the aircraft.

Air Vice Marshal Walker had previously flown to Melsbroeck to organise this operation. He also flew on 3 petrol missions on the 25th September, 28th September and the 2nd October, 1944.

26th September, 1944

21 aircraft to Brussels with load as before plus one from Woodbridge.

One aircraft was damaged on landing when wing tip hit the ground in gusty weather.

27th September, 1944

23 aircraft to Brussels with load as before.

28th September, 1944

23 aircraft to Brussels with load as before.

Station visited by 2 Officers and 30 other ranks from the Kings Royal Rifle Corps.

29th September, 1944

24 aircraft with load as before. One remained at Brussels with unserviceable hydraulics.

30th September, 1944

30 aircraft with load as before. One remained at Brussels with unserviceable hydraulics.

The Station Strength at the end of the month was:-

	OFFICERS	N.C.O.'s & AIRMEN
R.A.F.	163	1,357
R.C.A.F.	6	19
R.N.Z.A.F.	5	3
R.A.A.F.	10	28
W.A.A.F	15	317
Total	199	1,724
	1,923	

1st October, 1944

23 aircraft with load as before. One returned early with engine trouble and one remained at Brussels.

2nd October, 1944

22 aircraft with load as before.
In all, 70 aircraft of 4 Group delivered about 325 000 gallons of petrol to Brussels. This was about the same as the amount of fuel consumed by the aircraft.

6th October, 1944

Schloven. (Synthetic Oil Plant). 23 aircraft. One returned early with hydraulic trouble and was unable to raise undercarriage. Bombing well concentrated. 3 large explosions seen. Smoke rose to 4-5 000 ft. Main force of attack was to the West of the aiming point.

Opposition intense both en route and at the target. 16 aircraft damaged. No fighter opposition but 2 believed jet aircraft seen. Fighter escort of Spitfires and Mustangs.

7th October, 1944

Cleve. 24 aircraft. One returned early with hydraulics unserviceable. Photographs showed excellent results. Smoke rising to 12-13 000 ft. and large mushroom shaped cloud over 10 mile area visible from the French coast, 150 miles away.

Moderate to intense flak at target, 2 aircraft damaged and 2 seen shot down.

One aircraft had brakes fail on landing probably due to faulty gauge. Had to swing aircraft to avoid civilians at the end of the runway and hit a parked van.

9th-10th October, 1944

Bochum. 20 aircraft. 17 bombed on ground markers and 3 on sky markers. Results therefore depended on the accuracy of the markers and this was not a successful attack.

Flak was quoted as "not being up to Ruhr Standard" but 5 aircraft received flak damage and one had a rocket fired at it which missed.

One flak damaged aircraft was also attacked by a fighter but by "Magnificent Airmanship" landed at Manston with the wireless operator, W/O Bond wounded.

11th October, 1944

17 aircraft stood by for an attack on an unspecified target which was cancelled.

12th October, 1944

Gelsenkirchen. 23 aircraft. Cancelled at 16.45.

14th October, 1944

Duisburg. 25 aircraft. 2 returned early one with an oil leak and the other with oxygen trouble. This daylight operation was the start of Operation Hurricane. "To demonstrate to the enemy in Germany generally the overwhelming superiority of the Allied Air Forces in this Theatre".

Bombing was however scattered and although opposition was light 7 aircraft were damaged. No enemy aircraft seen. Fighter escort.

14th-15th October, 1944

Duisburg. 22 aircraft. Very successful attack. The whole target was a mass of flames visible 120 miles away. A spectacular explosion was also seen.

En route to the target one aircraft collided with another Halifax over the Dutch coast, both proceeded to the target as only minor damage was caused.

Opposition was slight. On return 15 aircraft had to land away.

A total of 1 005 aircraft took part in this raid. Duisburg had received a total of about 9 000 tons of bombs over 48 hours.

15th-16th October, 1944

Wilhelmshaven. 14 aircraft. Crews reported attack successful. Moderate flak in target area. One aircraft had an indecisive combat and 3 more fighters were seen. Searchlights ineffective owing to cloud and mist. Fires visible 50-60 miles after leaving the target.

17th October, 1944

Lecture given to all personnel on "The War in the Far East".

18th October, 1944

21 aircraft were detailed for an attack on Essen on the morning of the 19th October, 1944.

19th October, 1944

Operation to Essen cancelled at 04.50.
S/O Holland inspected W.A.A.F. Personnel.

21st-22nd October, 1944

Hannover. 13 aircraft. Re-called owing to deteriorating weather over England.

Kattegat. (Minelaying). 10 aircraft. 3 took off but were also re- called owing to deteriorating weather.

22nd October, 1944

An operation to Essen with 15 aircraft was cancelled.

22nd-23rd October, 1944

Kattegat. (Minelaying). 10 aircraft. All laid mines successfully.

Slight flak from flak ships. 2 enemy aircraft seen but no combats.

On return all aircraft landed at Full Sutton as Base Drem Lighting was U/S.

23rd-24th October, 1944

Essen. 25 aircraft. 2 returned early both with engine trouble. No results observed owing to 10/10 cloud.

Fairly accurate heavy flak, one aircraft damaged. 3 night fighters seen and one aircraft had an inconclusive combat.

This raid was the heaviest on Essen of the whole war and the number of aircraft dispatched-(1055) was a record in spite of 5 Group Lancasters not being involved.

24th October 1944

Operation to Essen with 20 aircraft cancelled at 1500 hours.

25th October, 1944

Essen. 24 aircraft. Bombed on flares due to heavy cloud. Master Bomber clearly heard. This attack, together with those of the 23rd and 24th October caused considerable damage.
Flak intensive at the start of the attack but lessened by the time the third wave came in. No enemy aircraft seen. Fighter escort of Spitfires and Mustangs. 2 aircraft returned on 3 engines.

27th October, 1944

Operation to Hannover, with 22 aircraft cancelled.

28th October, 1944

Cologne. 22 aircraft. 6 returned early due to "coring" of engines. This was caused by oil in the radiator congealing and therefore causing the engine to overheat. Most crews bombed visually but scattered cloud obscured target. This raid was reported as scattered but later research showed "enormous damage".
Intense flak at the target. No enemy aircraft.

30th-31st October, 1944

Cologne. 18 aircraft. One returned early with engine trouble. Target obscured by cloud, crews reported attack well concentrated round sky markers. This attack like the one on 28th October was at first thought to be scattered but these two attacks were later found to have done considerable damage.

The Squadron Operations Record Book for this month concludes "Although several aircraft damaged by flak no aircraft lost and nobody killed. In all probability this is a record for the Squadron. It says much for the training and co-operation of the aircrews and for the thorough work of the servicing personnel that this was so".

31st October-1st November, 1944

Cologne. 13 aircraft. One returned early with Gee and Intercom unserviceable. All crews saw sky markers and reported bombing well concentrated. One aircraft hit by incendiaries from another aircraft injuring 2 of the crew.

One rocket propelled aircraft seen.

2nd-3rd November, 1944

Dusseldorf. 21 aircraft. One returned early with engine trouble. Extensive fires seen at target and one large explosion. This was the last major raid of the war on Dusseldorf and considerable damage was done.
Flak intensive but mostly below our aircraft.

One aircraft was attacked by another Halifax over Belgium and then by a JU 88. The crew were ordered to bale out and 4 did so successfully but the Pilot Captain Begbie (S.A.A.F.) the Flight Engineer, Sgt. Jauncey and the Bomb Aimer F/O Warden were killed when the aircraft crashed near Louvain.

Another aircraft was attacked by an ME 110 but claimed it as damaged and a third aircraft was hit by incendiaries from another aircraft which caused a fire in the fuselage. "The Gunner and Flight Engineer showed great coolness in extinguishing the fire".

One aircraft failed to return.

LW 141 (U)

F/O Redmond Killed.
P/O Lemmon Prisoner of War.
P/O Picken Killed.
F/S Wilson Killed.
P/O Binstead Killed.
P/O Pearmain Killed.
Sgt. Lightfoot Killed.

3rd November, 1944

Bochum. 12 aircraft. Cancelled at 13.20.

4th November, 1944

Performance of "The Wind and the Rain" given by the Station Theatre Company.

4th-5th November, 1944

Bochum. 16 aircraft. 2 aircraft were forced to jettison after "hang up". Fires could be seen up to 80 miles away before the target was reached. The attack was well concentrated with an area of about one square mile on fire. A large explosion was also seen.

Flak fairly intensive. One aircraft slightly damaged. 2 aircraft had inconclusive combats with night fighters.

One aircraft failed to return.

MZ 772 (Q)

F/O Cameron Killed.
F/O Hudson Killed.
F/O Frobisher Killed.
F/O Bolton Killed.
Sgt. Wilby Killed.
Sgt. Swarft Killed.
Sgt. Jones Killed.

6th November, 1944

Gelsenkirchen. 18 aircraft. One returned early with engine unserviceable. Most aircraft able to bomb visually and bombing appeared well concentrated with a large fire in built up area.

One aircraft was hit by flak on the way to the target damaging the fuel system and causing an estimated fuel loss of 15 gallons a minute. This aircraft landed at Manston with brakes and fuel system unserviceable.

Although flak was described as moderate, 5 other aircraft were damaged. No enemy aircraft seen.

7th November, 1944

Lecture given by F/L Gerrard on "The Far East".

8th November, 1944

Minelaying operation to Oslo Fiord with 12 aircraft cancelled at 16.00.

9th November, 1944

Bombing operation to Julich with 6 aircraft cancelled. Aircraft being ferried to Woodbridge swung on take off tearing off undercarriage.

10th November, 1944

A bombing operation to Julich with 6 aircraft and a minelaying operation to the Kattegat area with 12 aircraft were both cancelled.

11th-12th November, 1944

Kattegat. (Minelaying). 12 aircraft. 2 brought mines back as H2S U/S. The rest were successful but one aircraft reported a large explosion as mine hit water. Was presumed to have fallen on a mine dropped by previous aircraft.

15th November, 1944

Gelsenkirchen. 18 aircraft. Cancelled at 23.35.

16th November, 1944

Julich. (Support for American Army). 21 aircraft. 2 returned early one with hydraulic trouble and the other with port inner unserviceable. Crews were able to bomb visually. Well concentrated and successful attack.

Moderate flak in target area, 2 aircraft slightly damaged and one badly with mid upper gunner wounded in the legs. This aircraft landed at Woodbridge. Fighter escort provided, no enemy aircraft seen.

17th November, 1944

Operation to Julich cancelled at 06.40.

18th November, 1944

Munster. 18 aircraft. One returned early with port outer on fire. Markers scattered so most crews bombed on "Navigational Aids". No results seen as target obscured by cloud.

Moderate flak. No enemy aircraft seen. Fighter escort.

On return one aircraft undershot landing at Carnaby writing off undercarriage.

Station visited by Assistant Chaplain in Chief Rev. Leslie Wright.

19th November, 1944

Operation with 18 aircraft to an Oil Plant cancelled at 13.15. (This target is not readable in the Operations Record Book but could be Homburg).

20th-21st November, 1944

Homburg. (Oil Plant). 21 aircraft. Cancelled at 16.45.

21st-22nd November, 1944

Sterkade. 15 aircraft. One returned early with engine trouble, overshot on landing and blocked main Hull/York Road for several hours.

Markers scattered at first but later concentrated, results could not be seen owing to clouds and smoke. The main target - the Oil Refinery was not hit.

Slight flak. No night fighters.

One aircraft (Capt. P/O Bailey) on last operation of tour had an engine fail on the way to the target, jettisoned part of the load, carried on with 3 engines and completed the operation.

Oslo Fiord. (Minelaying). 8 aircraft. Successful operation.

22nd November, 1944

Dortmund. 20 aircraft. Cancelled at 16.45.

23rd November, 1944

Dortmund. 19 aircraft. Cancelled at 15.10.

24th November, 1944

Dortmund. 19 aircraft. Cancelled at 16.40.

25th November, 1944

Essen. 19 aircraft. Cancelled at 12.00.

26th November, 1944

Aschaffenburg. 19 aircraft. Cancelled at 18.00.

27th-28th November, 1944

Oslo Fiord. (Minelaying). 6 aircraft. One returned early with starboard outer unserviceable.

Successful operation with negligible opposition.

28th-29th November, 1944

Essen. 26 aircraft. One returned early with starboard inner unserviceable. Markers well concentrated at first but scattered later. Results not observed owing to 10/10 cloud.

Slight flak in the target area and one twin engined enemy aircraft fired on.

30th November, 1944

Duisburg. 23 aircraft. 10/10 cloud over target but glow of intense fire could be seen. At first this attack was not considered to have been a success but later was found to have caused much damage.

Flak moderate. No night fighters.

The Station strength at the end of the month was:-

	Station HQ			102 Squadron			
	Aircrew	Ground Crew		Aircrew		Ground Crew	
	Officers	Airmen	Officers	Airmen	Officers	Airmen	Officers
R.A.F.	22	5	55	1,165	87	232	1
R.C.A.F.			1	4	24	13	
R.N.Z.A.F.					9	15	
R.A.A.F.					5	2	
S.A.A.F.					6		
W.A.A.F.			10	304			

A Total of 220 Officers and 1,740 Airmen. 1,960 Altogether.

2nd-3rd December, 1944

Hagen. 20 aircraft. 2 returned early with engine trouble. All bombed on "Navigational Aids" as markers could not be seen. No results observed but this was later found to have been a successful attack.

Opposition very slight. Few fighters seen but no combats.

5th-6th December, 1944

Soest. 22 aircraft. Attack well concentrated until the end when markers become a little scattered. At the end of the raid an area roughly conforming to the shape of the town and marshalling yards was on fire and burning furiously.

Opposition slight at first, then increased only to tail off towards the end of the attack. Few fighters seen. No combats.

On return one aircraft hit a tree due to unserviceable altimeter, this damaged the nose, flaps and H2S blister but this aircraft landed successfully at Carnaby.

6th-7th December, 1944

Osnabruck. 21 aircraft. One was forced to jettison near the target as all "Navigational Aids" and the Navigators Oxygen had gone unserviceable. Weather very bad. Heavy cloud and static reported by all crews.
No markers seen nor was the Master Bomber heard, so bombing was done on "Navigational Aids" and this resulted in a successful attack.

Moderate flak in the target area. One fighter seen but no combat.

9th December, 1944

An attack on the Urft Dam near Heim Bach was cancelled at 05.20 on the 10th December, 1944.

10th December, 1944

A further attack on the Urft Dam for the morning of 11th December, 1944 was cancelled at 23.05.

11th December, 1944

17 aircraft detailed to bomb Bielefeld and 5 aircraft for mining in the Kattegat. The minelaying operation was cancelled at 14.00 and the bombing at 15.00.

12th-13th December, 1944

Essen. 12 aircraft. One returned early with Gee unserviceable. Heavy cloud over the target forced aircraft to bomb on sky markers. Attack considered a success, 2 heavy explosions and large red glare seen in target area.

Crews reported the intense and heavy flak was up to 1943 Ruhr standard. 2 aircraft damaged by flak one of which was forced to land at Carnaby with hydraulic trouble.

(This was the last night raid on Essen of the war though 2 daylight raids were carried out in 1945).

13th-14th December, 1944

Oslo Fiord. (Minelaying). 6 aircraft. One brought mines back as Gee was unserviceable, the rest carried out a successful operation.

Some heavy flak at Oslo. Thick fog on return so all aircraft diverted to Dalcross.

This operation saw the end of the second operational tour of W/C L.D. Wilson D.F.C. A.F.C. the C.O. of No 102 Squadron.

14th December, 1944

Hannover. 16 aircraft. Cancelled at 13.25.

15th December, 1944

Dortmund. 16 aircraft. Cancelled at 13.25.

16th December, 1944

At the Services Drama Festival held at Leeds University. The Pocklington Theatre Company presented Act II of "The Wind and the Rain" and were adjudged winners by a substantial margin.

17th-18th December, 1944

Duisberg. 10 aircraft. Successful attack. There two aiming points one northern and one southern. 10 aircraft attacked each. Red glow seen through 10/10 cloud.

Opposition moderate. No fighters.

On return 2 aircraft forced to land at Carnaby with no brake pressure.

18th December, 1944

Cologne. (Koln Marshalling Yard). 18 aircraft. Cancelled at 13.25.

19th December, 1944

Hanau. 18 aircraft. Cancelled at 13.45.
Kattegat. (Minelaying). 6 aircraft. Cancelled at 16.45.

20th December, 1944

Cologne. (Koln Marshalling Yard). 16 aircraft. Cancelled at 16.45.

Kattegat. (Minelaying). 6 aircraft. Cancelled at 16.25.

21st-22nd December, 1944

Cologne. (Koln Marshalling Yard). 14 aircraft. This attack was curtailed. Only 5 aircraft actually took off. All aircraft forced to bomb on flares through solid cloud and this attack could not be considered a success, only a few bombs hitting the target.

All aircraft diverted on return due to weather.

Kattegat. (Minelaying). 6 aircraft. All successful but heavy flak from Aaborg damaged 3 aircraft.

As with the bombing operation all aircraft were diverted on return to Carnaby and Driffield.

22nd-23rd December, 1944

Bingen. 9 aircraft. This attack was curtailed. Only one aircraft took off and reported the attack appeared well concentrated at first but scattered later.

24th December, 1944

Mulheim Airfield. (Now Essen Municipal Airport). 24 aircraft. One returned early with engine trouble. Bombing well concentrated all over target area.

Heavy barrage flak both at target and en route. All aircraft diverted to Carnaby on return.

2 aircraft failed to return.

MZ 871 (G)

F/O Roberts Killed.
P/O Lea Prisoner of War.
P/O Ball Prisoner of War.
F/S Murphy Prisoner of War.
F/S Williams Killed.
Sgt. Simpson Killed.
F/S Steggell Prisoner of War.

LW 168 (O)

P/O Hislop Killed.
P/O Hawthorne Prisoner of War.
F/S Lindenboom Killed.
F/S Clements Prisoner of War.
Sgt. Worthing Prisoner of War.
Sgt. Temple Prisoner of War.
Sgt. Coupe Prisoner of War.

26th December, 1944

St. Vith. (German Troop Positions). 6 aircraft. This attack was on reinforcements for the German advance in the Ardennes. Thick smoke prevented observation of results but later photographs showed this was a successful attack.

Only slight opposition. On return all aircraft were again diverted to Carnaby.

28th-29th December, 1944

Munchen Gladback. 17 aircraft. Bombed through 10/10 cloud. No results observed and in fact little damage was done.

Negligible opposition. One aircraft forced to land at Woodbridge with low brake pressure.

29th December, 1944

Koblenz. 16 aircraft. This attack completed the damage to the railway facilities following a U.S.A.F. attack the previous day. Bombing scattered, Master Bomber could not be heard as one aircraft had it's transmitter switched on.

Accurate flak at target. 4 aircraft damaged and one was forced to land at Manston with the Navigator P/O C. J. Forrester wounded in the leg. No enemy aircraft seen.

30th-31st December, 1944

Cologne. (Kalk Marshalling Yard). 16 aircraft. All bombed the target through heavy cloud. No results seen except for increasing glow through cloud. One crew reported good fire approximately 5 miles square, but later reports showed the attack had been a considerable success, at least 2 ammunition trains blew up.

Some aircraft reported dummy sky markers west of Dusseldorf.

The Medical Officer reported for the month that the general health of the Station remained good. He also commented on the complete lack of in-patients over the Christmas period.

The Station strength at the end of December, 1944 was:-

| | Aircrew | | Groundcrew | |
	Officers	Airmen	Officers	Airmen
R.A.F.	121	178	60	1277
R.C.A.F.	1	12		4
R.A.A.F.	20	12		
R.N.Z.A.F.	8			
S.A.A.F.	3			
W.A.A.F.			9	342
Totals	153	202	69	1623

A Total of 222 Officers and 1,825 Airmen.   2,047.

THE LOST

Think of them. You did not die as these
Caged in an aircraft that did not return
Whenever hearts have song and minds have peace
Or in your eyes the pride of banners burn
Think of these who dreamed and loved as you
And gave their laughter, gave their sun and snow
Their English grave blessed by their native dew
That you would live. To them this debt you owe
Their glory shines about the sky forever
Though in the things they left to you, the ghost
Should haunt your field of ease and resting river.
Their lives are ended, but dreams are not yet lost
If you remember in your laugh and song
These boys who do not sing and laughed not long.

Herbert Corby.

(From "The Terrible Rain" published by Methuen Co.).

1945

On the 9th May 1945 all the German forces surrendered and following the atomic bombs on Hiroshima and Nagasaki the Japanese surrendered on the 14th August.

The full horror of Nazism was now revealed with the overrunning of the concentration camps especially Belsen and Dachau. How many people died in these camps will never be known but it must run into several million.

February saw the most controversial raid of the whole war when Dresden was wiped out. At first it was thought that the death toll on this raid was about 130,000 but later research has put the figure at 45,000. The Americans with their new long range B 29's were now devastating Japan. One firestorm raid on Tokyo alone was estimated to have killed 84,000 people.

1st-2nd January, 1945

I have been informed by several people that at about 05.00 a V.1 which had been air launched from the North Sea landed on the west side of the airfield near Barmby Moor destroying a Halifax aircraft. There is no trace of this in the Station records. It appears that this V.1 landed just outside the airfield boundary at the Barmby Moor end of the field at the site now occupied by a warehouse.

Dortmund. (Benzol Plant). 11 aircraft. The Pathfinders were late and this resulted in a scattered attack. The Benzol Plant was not hit. One aircraft overshot the target and bombed Vohinkel the target of 3 Group Lancasters.

On return one aircraft hit a house at Riverhead 700 yards from the runway. The Bomb Aimer F/S Sheridan was killed and the Pilot F/L Langham badly injured. The rest of the crew were only slightly hurt. The rapid response of the fire party to this incident was noted.

2nd January, 1945

One aircraft overshot on landing. Swung aircraft to avoid running off the end of the runway and collapsed undercarriage.

2nd-3rd January, 1945

Ludwigshaven. 18 aircraft. One returned early with engine unserviceable. One aircraft with crew on first operation bombed decoy markers. This attack was well concentrated. 2 large explosions seen and considerable damage done.

Opposition intense at first but slackened off as attack developed.

5th-6th January, 1945

Hannover. 20 aircraft. This was the first large raid on this target since October 1943 and was to complete the destruction of the town together with rail facilities and industry.

Crews bombed on sky markers as ordered by Master Bomber. Glow of fires seen through cloud.

Opposition more intense than of late. Numerous fighter flares seen.

3 aircraft failed to return.

LL 597 (X)

F/L Jones Prisoner of War.
Sgt. Day Prisoner of War.
F/S Wilson Prisoner of War.(Wounded).
Sgt. Shaw Killed.
Sgt. Harding Killed.
F/S English Killed.
Sgt. Frankling Killed.
W/O Jones Killed.

MZ 756 (M)

F/O Bergman Prisoner of War.
F/O Smith Killed.
F/O Dale Prisoner of War.
F/S Stevens Killed.
Sgt. Aune Killed.

NL 502 (Y)

Capt. Heiden Killed.
F/S Quill Killed.
P/O Boorman Prisoner of War.
F/S Valery Killed.
Sgt. Jones Killed.
Sgt. Johns Killed.
W/O Tyler Killed.
Sgt. Morgan Killed.

F/S Dunphy Killed.
P/O Shirley Killed.

6th-7th January, 1945

Hanau. (To destroy built up area and associated industries). 17 aircraft. Crews again forced to bomb through 10/10 cloud and results not observed. This attack was later found to be scattered but many bombs did fall in the vicinity of the Railway Junction.

Opposition slight to moderate. Some enemy aircraft seen but no combats.

One aircraft had gun in mid upper turret go off twice for no apparent reason damaging the rear turret on the second occasion.

7th January, 1945

A bombing operation to Krefeld with 12 aircraft was cancelled at 13.10.

8th January, 1945

Duisburg. 15 aircraft. Cancelled at 23.30 due to weather.

12th-13th January, 1945

Kiel Bay. (Minelaying). 5 aircraft. All successful. Slight flak. Fighter flares seen but no combats.

Duisburg. 15 aircraft. Cancelled at 23.30 due to weather.

13th-14th January, 1945

Saarbrucken (Railway Yards). 21 aircraft. Markers well concentrated. Crews were able to identify river and built up area on run in. Attack well concentrated at first but scattered later.

Slight flak. No fighters.

14th January, 1945

W/C E.F.E. Barnard took Command of No 102 Squadron.

14th-15th January, 1945

Dulmen. 19 aircraft. One returned early after port outer cut on take off. It jettisoned load and landed at Carnaby. This attack on a fuel dump near Munster was disappointing. Markers badly scattered. Flak negligible.

16th-17th January, 1945

Magdeburg. 13 aircraft. 2 returned early one with undercarriage trouble and the other with intercom unserviceable. The first crews over the target could distinguish river and built up area but this later became obscured by smoke. Considered to have been a successful attack. Fires could be seen for a considerable distance after leaving the target.

Flak moderate. Fighter flares seen but no combats. One aircraft damaged in a collision over the target.

One aircraft failed to return.

LW 179 (Y)

S/L Jarard (C. Flight Commander) Killed.
P/O Davies Killed.
P/O Carter Killed.
W/O Galbraith Killed.
F/S Telfer Killed.
Sgt. Wilson Killed.
Sgt. Pope Killed.

Kattegat. (Minelaying). 6 aircraft. One brought mines back as Gee and H2S unserviceable. Rest were successful.

19th January, 1945

Bombing operation to Mainz cancelled.

21st January, 1945

Bombing operation to Mainz with 19 aircraft cancelled.

23rd-24th January, 1945

Gelsenkirchen. 17 aircraft. One returned early with starboard outer on fire. All bombed on fires and markers seen through low cloud. No results observed except for increasing glow through cloud. Flak heavy at first but lessened.

23rd January, 1945

Boxing Tournament held.

24th January, 1945

R.A.F. Gang Show entertained troops for 1.1/2 Hours.

27th January, 1945

Krefeld. 15 aircraft. Cancelled at 16.30.

28th-29th January, 1945

Stuttgart. (To destroy rolling stock and facilities and stop military movement). 15 aircraft. Adverse winds delayed aircraft and lack of flares forced many crews to bomb alternative targets after leaving the target area or jettison.

Opposition slight. No enemy aircraft seen.

Only 4 aircraft landed at base on return. The rest had to be diverted to airfields in the south of England.

29th January, 1945

Bombing operation to Mainz cancelled.

The Medical Officer reported that the health of the Station remained good in spite of the severe weather.

1st-2nd February, 1945

Mainz. 16 aircraft. One returned early with starboard inner unserviceable. Weather was 10/10 cloud over the target but a small break at the start of the attack enabled 3 crews to bomb on ground markers. However, the rest were forced to use sky markers. These were scattered at first but concentrated later. Crews reported glow of large fires seen but this attack was not a success as most of the bombs fell outside the Town.

Opposition slight. No night fighters seen.

2nd-3rd February, 1945

Wanne Eickel. 13 aircraft. 10/10 cloud over the target. Only a few crews saw markers the rest bombed on Gee. Glow of fires and large explosion seen but attack generally scattered.

Flak moderate but accurate, one aircraft damaged. One night fighter seen but no combat.

3rd-4th February, 1945

Elbe Estuary. (Minelaying). 8 aircraft. All laid mines accurately from H2S fixes. Uneventful trip but slight accurate flak encountered.

4th-5th February, 1945

Bonn. 16 aircraft. 10/10 cloud over the target but a break towards the end of the attack allowed 3 crews to see the ground markers which were spread over a 3 mile area but most crews bombed on the glow of markers through cloud. One aircraft attacked alternative target as no markers were seen. This attack was as a result badly scattered.

Opposition moderate. Some heavy barrage flak mostly below. Some fighters seen, one inconclusive combat.

5th-6th February, 1945

A bombing operation to Leipzig with 14 aircraft was cancelled at 19.15 on the 5th February, 1945.

7th February, 1945

G/C D.O. Young, D.S.O. D.F.C. A.F.C. took over as Station Commander.

7th-8th February, 1945

Goch. 17 aircraft. 2 returned early both with unserviceable engines. This attack was to prepare the way for XXX Corps across the German Frontier at Reischwald. This operation curtailed by the Master Bomber as smoke had obscured the target and 8 aircraft were forced to jettison. This attack however, did considerable damage.

Many fighters seen and one aircraft claimed to have destroyed an ME 410 which was seen to break up in the air and pieces hit the ground. All crews reported AA fire from our own defences.

2 aircraft failed to return.

LW 142 (N)

F/O Smallwood Killed.
F/S Russell Killed.
F/O James Killed.
F/S Hewitt Killed.
Sgt. Lennon Killed.
Sgt. Scott Killed.
Sgt. Gallagher Killed.

The second aircraft was attacked by an unidentified aircraft. The Captain W/O Smith ordered all the crew to bale out which they did successfully but was unable to abandon the aircraft himself and was killed.

8th-9th February, 1945

Kadet Channel. (Minelaying). 4 aircraft. Cancelled at 14.00.

9th-10th February, 1945

Bremen. 10 aircraft. Cancelled at 16.30.

River Weser. (Minelaying). 4 aircraft. Cancelled at 16.30.

10th-11th February, 1945

Dortmund. 14 aircraft. Cancelled at 15.45.

11th-12th February, 1945

Dortmund. 14 aircraft. Cancelled at 16.50.

13th-14th February, 1945

Bohlen. 17 aircraft. One returned early with starboard outer unserviceable. Cloud 8/10 over the target. Master Bomber clearly heard and markers seen. Glow of fires and large explosion but attack generally scattered.

Moderate heavy flak in target area. 4 fighters seen but no combats.

On return, 8 aircraft landed at Mepal, 2 at Manston and one at Melsbroeck due to fuel shortage.

14th-15th February, 1945

Chemnitz. (Now known as Karl Marx Stadt). One aircraft. No instructions from Master Bomber but bombing appeared well concentrated. Later reports showed this city spared the worst results of its first major R.A.F. raid.

Slight heavy flak.

Kadet Channel. (Minelaying). 4 aircraft. All successful.

15th-16th February, 1945

Horten. 6 aircraft. (Minelaying). All laid mines on H2S fixes. Opposition slight, accurate flak from Horten. No enemy aircraft seen. All aircraft diverted to Peterhead on return.

17th February, 1945

Wesel. 8 aircraft. Not a successful operation. Master Bomber could only be faintly heard and after calling crews down to 10, 000 ft. could still see nothing.

Operation abandoned and aircraft brought bombs back only to be diverted due to weather.

20th-21st February, 1945

Dusseldorf. 7 aircraft. This attack on the small target of the Oil Refinery at Reisholz was at first thought to be a failure but it was later established that it had been accurate and the refinery ceased production.

One aircraft reported "A heavy explosion".

Night fighters active and several combats seen.

Several aircraft had to divert and one returned to base on 3 engines, to overshoot on landing, the crew however were unhurt. This aircraft unable to reach the target, had bombed Zissen.

This was the first operation with Halifax Mk. VI aircraft.

21st-22nd February, 1945

Worms. 12 aircraft. This was the only large attack on this city and caused considerable damage.

Opposition moderate. 2 inconclusive combats with night fighters.

23rd February, 1945

Essen. 7 aircraft. One returned early with starboard outer unserviceable. This attack took place in 10/10 cloud and was at first thought to be a failure. However, due to very accurate sky marking the Krupps Works was badly hit. Though the Pocklington aircraft bombed on Gee fixes the 342 aircraft involved hit the target with about 300 high explosives and 11 000 incendiaries.

One aircraft bombed Dusseldorf owing to unserviceable compass and H2S and one commented that the flak at the target was "Negligible in quantity but excellent in quality". No enemy fighters seen.

24th February, 1945

Kamen. 12 aircraft. All bombed on Gee through heavy cloud. The town was badly damaged but the main target, the Oil Plant at Berg Kamen was not hit. Negligible opposition.

27th February, 1945

Mainz. 16 aircraft. Master Bomber ordered sky markers which were well concentrated over a 2 mile square area in spite of 10/10 cloud. Considerable destruction caused and crews reported cloud over the target swelling in heat of fires.

Opposition slight but some accurate flak from Worms and Alzey. No enemy aircraft seen. Our own fighter escort stated to be "Very Efficient".

2nd March, 1945

Cologne. 16 aircraft. This was a daylight raid on Cologne now almost in the front line, with the intention of blocking the Rhine crossing and was a successful operation. All crews had a good glimpse of the river and town which was covered by smoke and dust when the attack ended. Spectacular fires and large explosions seen with smoke rising to cloud base. All No 102 Squadron aircraft bombed over a 3 minute period between 10.07 and 10.10.

No fighters seen and opposition only slight. (4 days later Cologne fell to American troops).

3rd-4th March, 1945

Kamen. 18 aircraft. One returned early unable to retract undercarriage. This raid was to complete the destruction of the Synthetic Oil Plant. The ground markers were clearly seen through thin cloud. Several large orange/red explosions observed and a large fire developed towards the end. The Oil Plant was badly damaged and no further production took place.

Opposition slight. 5 enemy aircraft seen and one aircraft had an inconclusive combat with a JU 88.

On return 4 aircraft had to land away owing to the presence of "Intruders" in the Pocklington area. (This was the night of the Luftwaffe Operation "Gisella" when a force of about 200 night fighters followed the bombers back to England to attack them over their own bases when they would be at their most vulnerable. 20 of our aircraft were shot down. 3 German aircraft crashed flying too low. One came down near Elvington. This was the last German aircraft to crash on British soil during the war).

5th March, 1945

Performance of "School for Husbands" given by Station Theatre Group. Repeated on 6th March, 1945.

5th-6th March, 1945

Chemnitz. 15 aircraft. One returned early with port outer unserviceable. This raid was "To complete the destruction of built up areas, industry and rail facilities". Results not observed due to cloud but red glow and several large explosions seen. One aircraft bombed Bonn owing to engine trouble.

Opposition at target light but Leipzig and Dorsten active.

Many fighter flares seen.

One aircraft failed to return.

RG 502 (Q)

F/O Hurley Killed.
F/S Briggs Killed.
F/O Valentine Prisoner of War.
Sgt. Smith Killed.
Sgt. Cooney Killed.
Sgt. White Prisoner of War.
Sgt. Morton Prisoner of War.

7th-8th March, 1945

Hemmingstedt. 5 aircraft. Markers clearly seen and attack well concentrated. Unfortunately the main weight fell 2-3 miles from the target.

Negligible opposition. No night fighters.

Kiel Bay. (Minelaying). 9 aircraft. Uneventful trip. No opposition although one aircraft seen to go down in the target area and 3 into the sea on the way back.

8th-9th March, 1945

Hamburg. 8 aircraft. One returned early with port inner unserviceable. This raid was to delay the production of the new Type XX1 U Boats. (These were equipped with a Schnorkel breathing tube and a new type of electric motor. They would have been a grave threat if the war had lasted much longer).

The markers were scattered and it was not possible to say if this was a successful attack. One spectacular explosion lasting 10-15 seconds seen.

Heavy flak, accurate but spasmodic. Several fighters seen but no combats.

River Elbe. (Minelaying). 5 aircraft. One returned early also with port inner unserviceable. 3 dropped on markers and the other on an H2S fix. Opposition slight.

9th-10th March, 1945

Hagen. 2 aircraft. Cancelled at 14.40.

Kattegat. (Minelaying). 8 aircraft. All laid mines accurately. Quiet uneventful trip.

11th March, 1945

Essen. 14 aircraft. (This raid is referred to as a Blitz Attack). No results observed owing to 10/10 cloud but a heavy mushroom shaped cloud was seen forcing its way through. The sky marking was however accurate and the bombing was well concentrated. This was the last raid on Essen which was now mostly in ruins.

Opposition slight. No enemy aircraft seen. Our own fighter escort well in evidence.

(This raid had the largest number of aircraft, 1 079 consisting of 750 Lancasters, 293 Halifaxes and 36 Mosquitoes sent to a single target so far in the war).

Reichswald Forest Memorial

12th March, 1945

Dortmund. ("Disorganise and destroy railway facilities, industry and remaining built up area in daylight Blitz"). 16 aircraft. All crews bombed sky markers on Master Bomber's instructions. One crew saw considerable glow under cloud and a smoke "mushroom" was seen forcing its way through cloud to 6-7 000 ft.

Opposition slight. Fighter escort.

(1 108 aircraft. 748 Lancasters, 292 Halifaxes and 68 Mosquitoes took part in this raid, a record which would stand to tne end of the war. Only 2 Lancasters were lost).

13th March, 1945

Wuppertal. ("Complete destruction of built up areas and railway facilities"). 17 aircraft. Markers late and only blue smoke puffs seen. Master Bomber clearly heard and instructions carried out. 3 crews reported fires and a large explosion.

Opposition light. No enemy aircraft. Fighter escort.

Over the last 3 days Bomber Command had flown 2 541 daylight sorties to the Ruhr, dropped about 10 650 tons of bombs, crippled 2 cities and one town, for the loss of 5 aircraft.

14th-15th March, 1945

Homberg. ("Block rail routes, destroy enemy troops and armour"). 13 aircraft. One returned early. This aircraft was unable to raise the undercarriage. This was followed by a fire in the starboard inner engine and failure of the port inner. Unable to climb above 800 ft., the bombs were jettisoned off Filey and an emergency landing made at Carnaby.

Markers short at first but later accurate and most bombs fell within 5-600 yards of the target. Fires at Zweibrucken which had been bombed by a force of 230 aircraft were reported to be getting a good hold.

Opposition slight. One night fighter seen.

15th March, 1945

Mathias Stinney. (Benzol Plant). 9 aircraft. Attack well concentrated. Smoke seen to cover whole of target area by the end of the attack and a large explosion was also seen.

Slight heavy flak at target but intense predicted flak in the Essen/Duisburg area.

One aircraft hit by flak losing fin, starboard rudder and jamming elevators. This aircraft crash landed at Manston and caught fire. The crew escaped unhurt.

18th-19th March, 1945

Witten. ("Complete destruction of built up area, rail facilities and industry"). 16 aircraft. Ground and sky markers clearly seen. Bombing scattered at first but later became more concentrated. Large explosions and fires seen to gain a good hold.

Opposition slight to moderate but some heavy flak.

Fighters seen. One inconclusive combat. Some aircraft reported seeing dummy ground and sky markers.

One aircraft failed to return. The last to be lost from Pocklington.

PP 179 (A)

Pilot F/O R.D. Jeff Killed.
Navigator F/S V.J. Sutherland Killed.
Air Bomber F/S W.N. Birkett Killed, Aged 21.
W/Operator Sgt. G.R. Grimsdell Killed, Aged 20.
Air Gunner Sgt. G.E. Emerson Killed.
Air Gunner Sgt. E.G. Hick Killed, Aged 25.
F/Engineer F/S J.G. Fraser Killed.

They are buried together with 3 971 other R.A.F. and Commonwealth Airmen in the Reichswald War Cemetery, Plot A, Graves 1-7. This Cemetery is situated between Kleve (Cleves) in Germany and Gennep in the Netherlands.

The aircraft crashed in the Bretchen area.

22nd March, 1945

Dulmen. (Enemy troops and supplies). 15 aircraft. Markers clearly seen and built-up areas visible. Bombing well concentrated. Large column of smoke rising to 6-7 000 ft.

Opposition negligible. No enemy aircraft.

24th March, 1945

Sterkade. ("Block lines and disorganise rail traffic"). 17 aircraft. Concentration appeared good with smoke rising to 8-10 000 ft. by the end of the attack.

Opposition negligible. No enemy aircraft.

W.A.A.F. Hockey team beaten by Swinderby 1-0 in Bomber Command Semi-Final.

Station Theatre Company terminated a successful tour of Stations in the Group with "School for Husbands".

25th March, 1945

Osnabruck. 15 aircraft. All crews identified the target visually. Markers soon obscured by smoke and Master Bomber ordered crews to bomb the centre of the smoke. Well concentrated attack.

Some heavy accurate flak. No enemy aircraft. Fighter escort well in evidence.

27th March, 1945

W/C D.F. Hyland Smith took Command of No 102 Squadron.

28th March, 1945

Station F.A. Team beat Snaith in the Final of 4 Group Trophy.

31st March, 1945

Mens Hockey Team reached the Final of 4 Group Trophy beating Driffield 2-1.

4th-5th April, 1945

Hamburg. ("To complete the destruction of the repaired and partly active Oil Refinery at Rhenavia"). 15 aircraft. Markers well concentrated and Master Bomber clearly heard but most crews were able to bomb visually by the light of photo flares and bomb bursts. Large explosion seen.

Opposition moderate. 2 aircraft had combats and one claimed a night fighter shot down. One aircraft had slight flak damage.

8th-9th April, 1945

Hamburg. ("Destroy Dockyards and Associated Buildings"). 14 aircraft. One had a "hang up" over the target and was forced to jettison. Master Bomber not heard by all crews, generally a scattered attack but some good explosions seen.

Some accurate heavy flak in the target area. No enemy aircraft.

On return one aircraft landed at Carnaby with low brake pressure.

9th-10th April, 1945

Flensburg. (Minelaying). 14 aircraft. One returned early with engine trouble. Successful operation except for one aircraft which dropped mines safe due to electrical failure. No opposition.

11th April, 1945

Nuremburg. 16 aircraft. One returned early with engine trouble. Target easily seen in good visibility and Master Bomber clearly heard. Accurate attack, large explosions seen with smoke cloud rising to 12 000 ft.

Opposition moderate. One aircraft damaged. Fighter escort (Mustangs) well in avidence.

11th April, 1945

Station Soccer Team reached Finals of York Senior Cup Half Holiday League.

Station Hockey Team reached the Finals of Group Hockey Trophy.

13th April, 1945

Flensburg. (Minelaying). 6 aircraft. All laid mines accurately with very little opposition.

On return, all aircraft diverted to the U.S.A.F. Base at Chelveston due to visibility.

18th April, 1945

Heligoland. (Guns and Military Installation). 20 aircraft. Clear over target with good visibility. Markers well placed and bombing well concentrated. Crews reported attack should be very successful.

Opposition negligible. Fighter cover well in evidence.

On return one aircraft found a large hole in the bomb doors. This was thought to be due to a bomb releasing inadvertently when the bomb doors were shut.

The Station Theatre Company presented a Musical Review "Punch Bowl". Repeat performances on the 20th and 26th April, 1945. Company then toured other Stations in the Group.

21st April, 1945

Ensa presented Comedy Thriller "Ladykiller".

25th April, 1945

Wangerooge. (Coastal Defence Guns). 19 aircraft. One returned early with starboard inner unserviceable. Attack accurate at first but target indicators became obscured by smoke causing bombing to be somewhat scattered later.

Opposition slight to moderate. No enemy aircraft.

When Halifax VI RP 171 (H) landed at 19.08 the last operation from Pocklington was over. The crew were:-

Pilot F/L J.W. Fowler.
Navigator F/O S. Brown.
Air Bomber F/O E.G. Wright.
W/Operator Sgt. A. Miller.
Air Gunner Sgt. J.H. Lewis.
Air Gunner Sgt. G. Fleet.
F/Engineer Sgt. J.A. Chamberlain.

This aircraft took off at 14.54. No cloud. Visibility good. Bombed visually at 17.05 hours heading 105°3T Knots. Target area obscured by smoke. 9 x 1 000 MC 4 x 500 AMM 64.

(This aircraft was subsequently sold to the Lancashire Aircraft Corporation as G.AKNL. This registration was cancelled on the 8th March, 1948 and the aircraft scrapped).

The Squadron Commander recorded in the Operations Record Book for No 102 Squadron. "Although it was clear that the Germans were all but beaten, few, if any, realised that the operation against Wangerooge on the 25th April, was actually to be our last. Our sword must now be beaten into a ploughshare and we look forward to playing a useful if less exciting role in Transport Command".

D.F. Hyland Smith,
Wing Commander,
No. 102 (Ceylon) Squadron,
R.A.F.

It is difficult to state exactly how many operations were flown or how many aircraft were lost from Pocklington but the following figures from Martin Middlebrook and Chris Everitt's masterly "Bomber Command War Diaries" gives a fairly accurate picture.

No 405 Squadron

During it's time in No 4 Group this Squadron flew 522 Wellington sorties for the loss of 20 aircraft. It also flew 396 Halifax sorties for the loss of 26 aircraft. A loss rate of 3.8 and 6.9% respectively.

During the war this Squadron flew 3,852 sorties for the loss of 112 aircraft. (2.9%).

No 102 Squadron

This Squadron started the war with Whitley's and suffered the third heaviest overall losses in Bomber Command along with No 44 and No 78 Squadrons. The Halifaxes flew a total of 4,734 sorties for the loss of 192 aircraft. A loss rate of 3%.

During the war this Squadron flew a total of 6,106 sorties for the loss of 192 aircraft. (3.1%).

Squadron personnel were awarded 6 D.S.O.'s 132 D.F.C.'s 3 Bars to D.F.C. and 36 D.F.M.'s.

Aircrew

Approximately 125,000 aircrew served in Bomber Command and nearly 60% became casualties.

Killed in Action or died while Prisoner of War	47,268
Killed in Flying or Ground Accidents	8,195
Killed in Ground Battle Action	37
Total Fatal Casualties	55,500
Prisoners of War (including many wounded)	9,838
Wounded in Aircraft which returned from operations	4,200
Wounded in Flying or Ground Accidents	4,203
Total Wounded	8,403

Over the whole war Bomber Command flew 389,809 sorties for the loss of 10,321 aircraft.

In spite of this at the end of the war no Campaign Medal was awarded to Bomber Command Aircrew and Air Chief Marshal Harris who had led Bomber Command through most of the war was ignored.

While these figures seem appalling, it must be remembered that on one day in 1916, 60,000 men died on the Somme for a few yards of French mud.

Aircrew selected for Bomber Command were expected to complete a tour of 30 operations before been rested, then a tour of a further 20.
The chances of survival from 50 operations was therefore as follows:-

Loss Rate % Survivors from 100 Crews

Loss Rate %	Survivors from 100 Crews
1.0	60.5
1.5	47
2.0	36.4
2.5	28.2
3.0	21.8
3.5	16.8
4.0	13.0

25th April, 1945

Dewsbury Theatre Society presented "Jack with Jills".

1st May, 1945

Driffield Concert Party presented "Hay Fever".

2nd May, 1945

Station visited by 3 Russian Radar Officers to study Halifax aircraft.

7th May, 1945

R.C.A.F. Concert Party presented "W. Debs".

8th May, 1945

V.E. Day. Commander G/C D.O. Young's D.S.O., D.F.C., A.F.C., Speech overleaf.

R.A.F. Pocklington together with other units in 4 Group transferred to Transport Command.

9th May, 1945

All Canadian personnel sent to Warrington for repatriation to Canada. It was recorded "That they have done their part right nobly".

All Air Gunners sent on indefinite leave.

GROUP CAPTAIN YOUNG'S SPEECH TO STATION PERSONNEL ON VE DAY

(8TH MAY, 1945).

On this great day, the day which marks the end in Europe of the greatest war that the world has ever seen, we must lift up our hearts and thank God for the present of victory. Five years ago today enemy forces were overrunning the whole of Western Europe and this small island was the only bulwark of Christianity left. Since then we have all suffered; some of us have lost our nearest and dearest relatives, some have had their homes destroyed by bombing and all of us have seen a great many of the best men of the country going out to fight and not coming back. We must thank God that this sacrifice has not been in vain.

I would like to thank you all, every single one of you for the great part you have played in achieving this great victory. When I tell you that in March, when everybody was worked until they were nearly dropping from lack of sleep, the two Flights of 102 Squadron dropped more bombs on Germany than any other two Flights in the whole of this Group, you will understand that your part has been and how proud I am to command this station during these weeks and months of victory.

Now the war in Western Europe is over and we no longer fear that our country will be over-run, we must remember the men of the Dominions, and Allies and Colonies who came to help us when we needed help so badly. Now we must do our utmost to help them to overcome the enemy on the other side of the world.

Today is a day of Thanksgiving and of celebration. We will celebrate it as best we can. Some of us obviously must remain on duty. I think you will understand that, but I shall ask every officer to release as many men and as many girls as they possibly can during the next two days to celebrate. This afternoon there will be games for those who wish to play them or to look on and to support them. Tonight, there will be a Victory Dance in the Station Dance Hall.

We will drink to our victory and play games and dance, but remember this, that a drunken man loses all dignity and self respect and brings disgrace upon the Service that even the Germans admitted has been the cause of the downfall of our enemies, and a drunken girl is the most deplorable and disgusting sight in the whole world. I can see that you agree with me.

Now there are many things I should like to tell you about the possibility of release from the Service. I am just out of sick bed and I am afraid I cannot stand up here to tell you the whole story. Some will still have to fight against our enemies overseas. Some will, in the course of the next few months, be released to civil life, but that release is bound to be slow and to be an ordered one. I want you to understand the difficulties and complications of releasing hundreds of thousands of people to civil life. It can't be done until civil life is ready to receive them, so now we will say a prayer and remember that we have not yet finished our work.

The day after VE day:- The Superintendant of Pocklington Police called on the Station Commander to congralulate him on the exemplary behavour of his personnel; stating that although extra precautions had been taken it had not even been necessary to check anybody.

10th May, 1945

Aircraft engaged in disposing of U/S bombs by dumping them at sea experienced control problems and was forced to ditch. No casualties.

23rd May, 1945

Aircraft being ferried to St. Athan overshot into a ditch.

The 'Red House'

28th May, 1945

First of a series of visits by Army ex Prisoners of War to the Station (It should be noted that numbers 1, 5 and 6 Groups had flown 75,000 ex P.O.W.'s back to England before the War finished, unlike the First War when some P.O.W.'s were not home by Christmas).

30th May, 1945

F/L Hart appointed Station Release Officer.

June 1945

Many trips done over Germany with Ground Crew as passengers to show them the results of their efforts.

A Dance was held on the 27th to celebrate the sixth Anniversary of the founding of the W.A.A.F. followed by a Parade and March Past on the 28th.

July 1945

Many more trips over Germany for Ground Crew including some W.A.A.F.'s who much appreciated seeing the results of their efforts. Sympathy was expressed for Dutch over the flooding of their country.

Main runway 14/32 became serviceable having been under repair for 7 weeks.
On the 20th July, a taxiing aircraft had its brakes fail. Swung off perimeter track and hit a parked aircraft.

On the 30th July, Halifax VI RG 482 crashed on the Red House on the edge of the airfield. Apparently one engine failed on take off and the pilot retracted the flaps instead of the undercarriage. All the crew were killed. There were fortunately no civilian casualties.
The Station Commander G/C Young took personal charge of the rescue party and burrowed under the ruins. The fire was not subdued until 20.00 and the bodies of F/L B. Dalmais, Sgt. R.D. Frost, Sgt. J. Milne, Sgt. W.H. Bradshaw and Sgt. R.L. Williams were not recovered until 21.45.

A considerable amount of sport was now being played. Cricket, Hockey, Soccer, Boxing, Swimming and Athletics.

4th August, 1945

Funeral of F/L B. Dalmais held at Pocklington.

5th August, 1945

Liberator aircraft arrived for local flying.

9th August, 1945

Highly successful Sports Meeting held at Pocklington School.

12th August, 1945

Station Church Parade held.

15th August, 1945

V.J. Day.

19th August, 1945

National Day of Thanksgiving. Large attendance at Voluntary Service in the Station Church.

27th August, 1945

Stirling aircraft started arriving for modifications and Dakotas from Holme on Spalding Moor for local flying.

At the end of the month it was reported that nearly all ground personnel had seen the destructive effect of Bomber Commands effort against Germany.

2nd September, 1945

G/C D.O. Young, D.S.O., D.F.C., A.F.C. the Station Commander was released from the Service and replaced by G/C J. Bradbury, D.F.C.

4th September, 1945

No 102 Squadron ordered to move to Bassingbourn by 8th September. Squadron Commander protested strongly at the short notice and stated this would have a detrimental effect on all personnel and adversely effect post war recruitment.

8th September, 1945

First road convoy left for Bassingbourn at 08.30. The aircrew left from Pocklington Station at 10.30 and the Ground Crews at 11.15. They were entertained by the Station Band which played "Old Lang Syne" as the trains left.

15th September, 1945

Battle of Britain Parade held.

21st September, 1945

Elvington Halifax being flown in for storage overshot the runway and blocked Hudsow Lane for many hours.

Many Halifaxes were flown in for storage during this month.

October 1945

About 130 Technicians arrived from Belfast to modify Stirling Aircraft.

Halifax Aircraft now being ferried to Kinloss for disposal.

The Station closed for night flying on the 11th October.

11th November, 1945

Remembrance Day Parade held on Station and personnel also took part in Parade in York.

15th November, 1945

First "Dining In" night held in Officers Mess. 63 present.

30th November, 1945

G/C Bradbury D.F.C. replaced as Station Commander by G/C A.C. Brown D.S.O., D.F.C.

Release from the Service now taking place rapidly. Station strength now 159 Officers and 1 000 N.C.O.'s and Airmen.

25th December, 1945

In the tradition of the Service the Officers served Christmas Lunch to the Airmen.

29th December, 1945

19 Stirling aircraft arrived for fire prevention modification.

4th January, 1946

Last Halifax to be ferried to Hooton Park for disposal left.

Party given for Officers Mess staff.

5th January, 1946

Colour Hoisting Parade recommenced.

Party held in Officers Mess for children of Station personnel. Toys (made on the Station) were distributed, 2 to each child "Hosts appeared to derive as much enjoyment as small guests and parents".

6th January, 1946

First Church Parade of the Year held.

9th January, 1946

Station Commander posted. Station Administration officer took over temporary command.

12th January, 1946

Q.G.H. (Controlled Descent through cloud), exercise held with a Lancaster from Full Sutton.

15th January, 1946

W/C C.E.S. Lockett posted in as Station Commander.

1st February, 1946

Station reverted to day flying only.

Irish personnel went on strike. Dissatisfied with dinner (No complaint from R.A.F. Personnel). Alternative meal provided. The original meal of Irish Stew was served the next day with a pastry crust and did not give rise to any complaints.

4th February, 1946

F/L Hart Officer in Charge of release left the Station on his own release from the Service. "He has rendered Sterling Service in this difficult job due to his quiet efficiency, tact and patience".

6th February, 1946

Search for Anson aircraft EG 113 missing on a flight from Rearsby to Melbourne. Ground search by 46 personnel and air search by Station Commander in Oxford aircraft. Nothing found.

7th February, 1946

Further fruitless search for Anson. (No trace has ever been found of this aircraft or its 5 occupants. S/L Perkins, F/L Ireland, F/L Lawrence D.F.C., W/O Crabtree and W/O Webb).

14th February, 1946

Investigation held by 4 Group Catering Officer into complaints of Irish. No grounds for complaint found but it was felt that R.A.F. personnel had just cause for complaint on feeding habits of Irish.

21st February, 1946

Groundsmens hut burnt down. Fire caused by A.M.W.D. Employee lighting paraffin lamp and setting fire to oil soaked floor.

1st March, 1946

Dance held in Officers Mess.

13th March, 1946

First weekly colour hoisting parade held.

25th March, 1946

Last Stirling to be modified tested by Mr. Douglas Cotton of Short Bros. It was anticipated that this will be the last test flight this well-known pilot will carry out.

26th March, 1946

Ferry flight formed for the disposal of Stirlings.

29th March, 1946

Last Irish personnel left.

2nd April, 1946

Ferry flight for disposal of Stirlings commenced operations.

3rd April, 1946

Complete litter sweep of Communal Site and Servicing Area used by Irish ordered by Station Commander. The entire Station was involved. Work commenced at 08.10 and was completed by 08.50.

4th April, 1946

At 16.45 hours during a violent storm a lightning strike at the intersection of 14/32 and 07/25 caused a large crater.

11th April, 1946

Capt. Armstrong of B.O.A.C. landed in a Dakota to report on the suitability of Pocklington as a base for the Tudor and Halifax aircraft of B.O.A.C.

1st May, 1946

Last Halifax (PP 171) left for Hawarden.

4th May, 1946

Notification that the Station was to close on the 15th June received.

S/L Baron posted in as Station Commander.

10th May, 1946

Closing down party to be formed on 20th May. To consist of about 70 personnel.

20th May, 1946

Collection held for St. Dunstans Week. Station Commander gave rides in Station Oxford at 2/6 (12.5p) a time.

24th May, 1946

Officers Mess Farewell Party held.

27th May, 1946

Other ranks dance held in aid of St. Dunstans.

The last entry in the Pocklington Operations Record Book reads:-

"Cricket:-

2 matches were played and won before the fixtures had to be cancelled owing to the closing down of the Station".

Pocklington remained an inactive location until 22nd March, 1965 when it was finally disposed of to the Ministry of Public Buildings and Works.

The home of No 102 (Ceylon) Squadron RAF and No 405 (Vancouver) Squadron RCAF No 4 Group Bomber Command During World War II From Where so many Gave Their Lives in the Cause of Freedom. This Memorial was Raised by Old Comrades to All Those Men and Women Who Served in Both Squadrons At This and Other Bases in War and Peace.